# Joy
### in a
# Roman
# Jail

**John Moran**

TO RETHA,
my loving wife, the mother of our children
and the best friend I have in the world besides Christ,
I affectionately dedicate this book.

# JOY IN A ROMAN JAIL

## Daily Devotional Studies in Philippians

## TABLE OF CONTENTS

# INTRODUCTION

*One of the most important of all the ingredients which foster personal effective Christian growth is a consistent, dynamic devotional life. Such an exercise must include a careful systematic study of the Word of God and a meaningful prayer life. It is my hope that JOY IN A ROMAN JAIL will aid the reader in his attempt to cultivate both.*

*Of the accusations that critics may level at the average fundamental/evangelical Christian, one of the most valid must be that he speaks so authoritatively of a book about which he knows so little. The fact is, to a large degree, our personal and family devotional times are not either constructed or conducted in a way that would contribute much to solving this problem.*

*JOY IN A ROMAN JAIL is a devotional work, written for lay people. It is designed to lead the reader in daily fifteen minute expositional studies through Paul's letter to the Philippians. The brief general prayer at the close of each section will serve as a simple guide to assist him in approaching God in personal prayer resulting from the day's study. It is my sincere hope, not only that the heart of the reader will be warmed devotionally, but that the mind will also be able to grasp intellectually the deeper truths which form the content of this epistle.*

*All Biblical quotations have been taken from the New International Version of the Scriptures published by Zondervan Bible Publishers unless otherwise indicated. All italics are mine.*

*I will offer praise to Christ Jesus if He will use this book to enrich the personal devotional lives of individual believers. I will be deeply gratified if husbands and wives find it useful in pulling them together to focus clearly on the unique caring and sharing relationship God intends for them to experience in Christ through mutual Bible study and prayer. I anticipate that whole families will find it helpful as a guide for family worship.*

How can proper recognition be rendered to all of the persons who have contributed to the well of writings and conversations from which one draws in order to prepare a work such as this? I have endeavored to give proper credit throughout the book to authors from whose works I have quoted. If I have failed to do so at any point, it has been by mistake and I ask for the patient indulgence of those deserving the acknowledgement. Others, from whom I have not quoted, have also exercised much influence on my thinking through their published books and materials. I have attempted to identify these writers and works in the bibliography at the close of the book. But how shall proper thanks possibly be rendered to all of those who have written nothing for publication, but who have shared lasting impressions upon me in formulating my philosophy of life, which most certainly becomes evident in this devotional? They are recorded in heaven. I cannot name them all—but my deep gratefulness to them is very sincere.

I want to express appreciation to the official church board of the Zion Missionary Church in Elkhart, Indiana, where I serve as Senior Pastor, for their openness to this project. Without such understanding, the work would have been much more difficult. My special thanks is given to LaVelle Wise for her consistent and patient dedication in typing and retyping the manuscript and preparing it for publication—and to Cheryl Moore and Fran Graber for their added help in typing some of the pages. I am also deeply indebted to Janice Pritchard for proofreading the manuscript and offering numerous valuable suggestions which have made the text more readable.

I gladly commit the final results of the influence of this devotional in the lives of readers to Jesus Christ, our Savior and Lord. To Him be praise and honor both now and forever in a world without end. Amen.

John Moran
September 1, 1983

# THE SETTING AND BACKGROUND (1:1-2)

### The Servants Who Sent This Letter (1:1A)
### The Saints Who Received This Letter (1:1B)
### The Salutation Which Introduces This Letter (1:2)

*WEEK 1: Sunday*
*READ: Philippians 1:1-9 (Read again verses 1-2)*

## THE SETTING AND BACKGROUND

Scholars characterize Paul's letter to the Philippians as "the epistle of joy" for it emanates a fundamental positive outlook. The words "joy" and "rejoice" bound from its pages repeatedly. This display of such buoyancy of spirit becomes even more significant when we recall that, at the time he penned these pages, Paul himself was confined in Rome, imprisoned for his faith. Jail would hardly seem the most likely setting to draw inspiration to draft an epistle of such joy! But Paul's ability to be happy and excited about his Lord was apparently not contingent upon the varying circumstances he experienced in life.

The Christians to whom this letter was originally written were citizens of Philippi, a city founded in 368 B.C. and named after Philip, the father of Alexander the Great. Situated at the crossroads between Macedonia and Asia, this namesake eventually emerged as a large commercial center. Having been conquered by the Roman armies, it became one of a number of "Roman Colonies." Veteran soldiers who had served their stint of army duty settled with their families in these towns. They enjoyed the distinction of being a part of a community which had become a "little fragment of Rome." Pride in their Roman citizenship flaunted itself as one of the predominant traits of these fortunate people.

It was upon this city in about 52 A.D. that Paul, with Silas, Timothy and Luke, converged to preach the good news of Jesus Christ. Here Paul and Silas sang their way through a night in jail (Acts 16:11-12, 25-34). But in spite of persecution, a small band emerged as believers in Christ and a church was born. About twelve years later Paul addressed the scroll containing these paragraphs to the Philippian congregation, which by this time had blossomed into a maturing assembly. Most scholars date the writing of the letter around 60-65 A.D.

The evidence drawn from the context of the letter makes clear that Paul wrote to these Christians at Philippi for at least six reasons:

1. To encourage them in the midst of trial (1:28-30).
2. To urge them toward Christian unity and obedience (2:1-18).
3. To clarify that Epaphroditus had become ill "because of the work of Christ" (2:25-30).
4. To warn against false doctrine (3:1-21).
5. To ask for reconciliation between two quarreling ladies of the congregation (3:2).
6. To thank the Christians for a special gift sent to him (3:16).

Our devotional studies over the next three days will focus on his opening salutation found in verses 1-2. Tomorrow we will note especially THE SERVANTS WHO SENT THE LETTER. On Tuesday we will consider THE SAINTS WHO RECEIVED THE LETTER. And on Wednesday we will look at THE SALUTATION WHICH INTRODUCES THE LETTER. Let us pray that the Holy Spirit will make these daily meditations very practical to us, and that the results will transform our lives for the better.

_PRAYER: Our heavenly Father, as we reflect daily on the teachings of this delightfully inspiring epistle, enlighten us to know how to allow the Holy Spirit to lead us in a joyful path. Help us to manifest that joy consistently in our everyday lives and may our positive attitude become so contagious that others will want to share such pleasure with us. We ask this in Jesus' name. Amen._

*WEEK 1: Monday*
*READ: Philippians 1:1-2 (note especially verse 1A)*

## THE SERVANTS WHO SENT THIS LETTER

Let us give our attention today especially to THE SERVANTS WHO SENT THIS LETTER. In verse 1 we read these opening words: "Paul and Timothy, servants of Christ Jesus, to all the saints in Christ Jesus at Philippi, together with the overseers and deacons . . ." The designating of Timothy as a fellow sender of this document is not to insinuate that he actually coauthored its writing. Paul is simply identifying him as one of the most respected of his co-workers. He names Timothy in his opening salutations in no less than six of his epistles (2 Corinthians, 1 & 2 Thessalonians, Philemon, Colossians, and here in Philippians). On at least three occasions he dispatched him to various congregations to perform special ministries (Corinth, Thessalonica and Philippi). We also know that Paul wrote two letters addressed specifically to this fellow laborer in the gospel, the second being one of his last (1 & 2 Timothy).

Timothy hailed from Lystra. On his first missionary journey Paul visited this city and, in spite of persecution, saw a great turning to Christ. Some scholars are convinced that Timothy himself was brought to faith at this time. We do know that by the time Paul returned to Lystra on his second tour the brethren of the church were praising the spiritual capabilities of this new young believer. Thus Paul enlisted Timothy to travel with him as his helper—and from that point on he is identified with the apostle as one of his colleagues (Acts 14:6-23; 16:1-5). Through the years he came to be Paul's most constant and loyal companion. The great apostle appealed to him for help more often than any other of his co-workers. Thus it was that Timothy accompanied Paul, Luke and Silas when they first journeyed to Philippi to preach the gospel, and so was well known to this congregation.

Paul, in our text, calls himself and Timothy *both* "servants of

Christ Jesus." The word rendered "servants" is the one which means "slaves." Catch it! Though Paul was older, the recognized leader and the writer of the letter, he related to Timothy as equal to himself—*both* were slaves of Jesus Christ! Dr. Lloyd Ogilvie relates an incident in his refreshing book, *Let God Love You*, of a pastor who attended a National Clergy Conference. At the close he spoke to one of the leaders: "It's not so much what you said . . . the new ideas or different insights . . . that hooked me. It was the way you people related to each other. I saw a quality of relationship . . . a style of openness and freedom . . . a willingness to love the other person with all his uniqueness and hang-ups. When I saw that, listened to it, tested it, felt it, tried to blast it apart to no avail, I knew what I was missing and why my faith was so ineffective. You have given me a viable alternative."[1] I am satisfied that the members of the Philippian church observed this same type of spirit being manifested between Paul and Timothy and the other members of that early missionary team as well!

We have given special consideration to THE SERVANTS WHO SENT THE LETTER. As we come more and more to esteem Paul for his spiritual contribution to the apostolic church, let us not overlook the genuine commendation due to men like Timothy (and also Luke and Silas), without whose faithful support Paul's ministry would have utterly failed! God bless their offspring forever!

*PRAYER: Lord, we acknowledge our need of the continual support and encouragement of our brothers and sisters in Christ. Bless especially those whose lives and ministries have helped mold us into the people we are. Keep us ever grateful for these dedicated and Spirit-filled "encouragers of faith," and help us to never forget their lasting influence for good upon us. We ask this through Christ, our Savior. Amen.*

---

[1]From *Let God Love You* by Lloyd John Ogilvie. Copyright. © 1978 by Word Books, p. 13. Used by permission.

## THE SAINTS WHO RECEIVED THIS LETTER

Yesterday we considered THE SERVANTS WHO SENT THIS LETTER. Today we will look more closely at THE SAINTS WHO RECEIVED THIS LETTER. Paul's opening statement clarifies that he did in fact consider the original recipients of this epistle to be "saints." He says, "Paul and Timothy, servants of Christ Jesus, *to all the saints in Christ Jesus at Philippi*, together with the overseers and deacons . . ."

What mental picture forces itself upon your mind when we bring into play that term "saint"? One who has been dead for many years? One who has been elevated to sainthood by the vote of a council? A white haired grandmother with an angelic look on her face? A high powered Christian who you feel "just couldn't ever sin"? Paul addressed this letter "to all the saints in Christ Jesus at Philippi." Suppose he could write another letter and address it to "all the saints in Christ Jesus" at *your* hometown or city—do you have reason to believe that you would get one?

Who, after all, is a saint? We will search the New Testament in vain to find even one reference which makes use of the term "saint" to portray a special spiritual rank of exceptionally mature Christians. This word depicts, rather, *all* persons who are "God's set apart property"! *All* who, by the new birth, belong to the spiritual family of God are constituted "saints"! They are "God's people"! They are "God's holy ones." You see, when a repentant sinner, matter not his soiled background, turns from his sin and trusts Jesus Christ as his Savior, that moment he becomes the Lord's person and God claims him as His own. He will, without doubt, have faults remaining which he must needs overcome and shortcomings with which he may struggle—but he is God's man! He is a saint!

This fact is beautifully illustrated in the lives of the initial converts at Philippi. The first to turn to Christ was Lydia, a high class religious lady, a seller of purple, an Asiatic businesswoman from Thyatira (a leading city in Asia). Hearing Paul preach, she repented and believed, and then promptly led her household to the Savior (Acts 16:14-15). Following Lydia's conversion, a young Greek slave girl began to dog the path of the missionaries, crying out after them (Acts 16:16-19). Paul, grieved in his spirit, cast out the demon and the young girl's life was completely transformed.

But the results of this miracle landed Paul and Silas in jail. While they were bound in prison stocks a rugged jailer stood guard over the prisoners. At midnight these Spirit-filled missionaries shocked their warden when they began a singspiration prayer meeting! Suddenly the floor began to tremble —earthquake! The jail doors flew open with a mighty force and the shackles fell from the arms and legs of the apostle and his co-worker. Certain the prisoners had escaped (which would have assured his own death), the guard unleashed the sword to commit suicide. But, thwarted by Paul's cry to halt, and cringing before the apostle, he begged, "Men, what must I do to be saved?" Paul's response: "Believe in the Lord Jesus and you will be saved—you and your household." He believed, and as a result, his whole household came to faith in Christ (Acts 16:25-34)!

In these first three converts at Philippi was represented a cross section of all who would ever repent and believe in that city—Asiatics, Greeks and Romans; rich, poor and middle-class; religious, demon-possessed and heathen! But, understand well, when that elite religious Asiatic businesswoman and that poor demon-possessed Greek slave girl and the practical down-to-earth heathen Roman jailer all truly believed on the Lord Jesus Christ, in that moment of faith *all* became "saints" in the sight of God! Notwithstanding their assorted backgrounds, they became God's separated people. All had much spiritual growing to experience, but they were saved! They were forgiven! They were regenerated! They were accepted! They were "saints"!

So Paul is addressing this letter to "all the saints in Christ Jesus at Philippi," and then adds, "together with the overseers and deacons." If any of the people at Philippi ought to be saints, I suppose it should be these! The overseer (bishop or elder) was the one who led the congregation, nearly the equivalent to the present-day pastor. The deacon cared for such ministries as would free the overseer for the ministry of the Word of God (such as caring for the sick, the widows and the poor). Though I doubt that Paul was entertaining any feelings of humor as he opened this epistle, the wording does prompt a chuckle. "To all the saints"—and lest there be any doubts about the "overseers" and the "deacons," he includes them also. This reminds me of the three primary boys who, before Sunday school, were comparing notes on their fathers. "Is your daddy a Christian?" asked the first. "No, he's a deacon," the second answered. To which the third, not to be outdone, responded, "Mine isn't either; he's the preacher!"

This letter is addressed to *all* of these saints who were at Philippi—and to all saints today. It is written for all of us who believe in Jesus to salvation. We, too, have become recipients of its truths. So let us study it carefully and respectfully for our own eternal good.

*PRAYER: Dear Father, we do not always feel like we are saints, but we want to! We thank You for Your forgiveness and cleansing. We thank You that through Christ You have accepted us. Help us to live our lives today—and always— with sainthood in view, that Christ may be truly glorified in us. We ask this for Jesus' sake. Amen.*

*WEEK 1:  Wednesday*
*READ:  Philippians 1:1-2 one final time (read again verse 2)*

## THE SALUTATION WHICH INTRODUCES THIS LETTER

We have spent three days focused on these first two verses, but important thoughts are couched in these few words which will help set the pace for the remainder of the entire epistle. On Monday we considered THE SERVANTS WHO SENT THE LETTER. Yesterday THE SAINTS WHO RECEIVED THE LETTER took our attention. Now today let us take a closer look at THE SALUTATION WHICH INTRODUCES THE LETTER. In verse 2 Paul says, "Grace and peace to you from God our Father and the Lord Jesus Christ."

Now when Paul refers to "grace" in this opening context, he is certainly alluding to a type of "graciousness" which includes more than initial saving grace. That of which he speaks here has more to do with keeping grace, growing grace, overcoming grace. It refers to grace for proper behavior in trying circumstances and good attitudes during times of suffering and trial. It most assuredly includes grace to effectively share with others the good news of Jesus Christ. The word basically refers to "the favor which God bestows on us quite apart from any merit."

"And peace . . ." Note the order of these words. Theologically and experientially, this sequence is correct. We would expect Paul to be so careful, wouldn't we? First grace. Then peace! Where the former is not being appropriated, the latter, of necessity, will be lacking also.

I believe again that the "peace" expressed here is more than the original tranquility and "ceasing of inner war" which results when one trusts Christ and is saved. Here is an ever-enlarging, encircling peace which accompanies a life that is lived in the grace of God. It is *not* necessarily an *automatic* outcome of being a Christian. This type of peace will only become an integral part of our lives as we choose to maintain positive attitudes toward the varying circumstances of everyday experience—and as we choose to continually draw upon and exercise the "grace" to which Paul refers in this statement.

One troubled Christian asked her friend, who always seemed to be so much at peace with God and herself, "Georgia, how do you do it? You always seem so peaceful and collected. What makes you so different from me?"

"Well," Georgia replied, "for years after I found my Savior, I was always troubled and 'on edge.' Much of my problem was that I couldn't sleep at night—I'd roll and toss and fret about my troubles. Then one day I read in the Bible, 'Behold, he that keepeth Israel shall neither slumber nor sleep.' Well! I said to myself, 'Now Georgia, there isn't any reason for both of you to stay awake all night. And since He's planning to stay awake anyway, you might just as well sleep.' I've been sleeping well and trusting God ever since." God bless the likes of Georgia!

Peter, in his first epistle, is even stronger than Paul concerning this duo of grace and peace. He says, "Grace unto you, and peace, be multiplied . . ." Or, "Grace and peace be yours *in abundance.*" When we became Christians by faith in Jesus, through the grace of God, we received peace—peace with God. But as we continue to walk with the Lord in faith, it is God's purpose that both grace and peace begin to increase and abound in our hearts and lives. He wants both to possess us more and more! This salutation, with its expression of Paul's concern for believers, is much in order for us today. Let us recognize and draw on His grace continually and live in His peace for Jesus' sake!

*PRAYER: Living God, we offer our praise to You for Your unmerited favor so freely given to us. We thank You that we may live in Your peace through Your grace. Help us today to know how to draw on Your grace in order to adequately meet the circumstances we will face. Give us inner peace that we will be able to be true "instruments of Your peace" to someone this day. Amen.*

WEEK 1: *Thursday*
READ: *Philippians 1:3-8*

## TRUE FRIENDS IN CHRIST

The majority of us can look back with gratefulness and happily declare that God in His mercy has brought into our lives a number of people who have helped make us better persons. And some of us are *especially* enriched in that our memories include one or two God-sent individuals who have entered our lives in a very special way during a time of crisis or sorrow or joy. They shared themselves with us—and we will be eternally appreciative, both to them and to God! Though our paths have taken different directions, that rare fellowship remains. Whenever we meet, it becomes a unique type of reunion. Doubly blessed are those who have such friends!

As we study this epistle it will become quite apparent that the Philippian congregation had become genuinely "one of a kind" to Paul. There were those in the church with whom he had formed a significantly deep bond of fellowship. This same feeling does not seem to come through in quite the same way in other letters. It had all begun twelve or thirteen years previous to the drafting of this book. Under the ministry of Paul and his missionary team, a high-class Asiatic businesswoman and her household, a lowly demon-possessed Greek slave girl and a common jailer and his family all came to saving faith in Jesus Christ. This small congregation began to grow and mature—

others were also converted—the evidence of truly changed lives was very practical and real.

Finally Paul went his way. But through the years they had "kept in touch." And now he is writing back expressing his deep appreciation for them as fellow saints.

I believe we see in this section the type of love and mutual respect that all fellow Christians ought to be striving to establish among themselves by the grace of God. For the next three days we will consider three expressions of that warmth of spirit which Paul possessed and conveyed to the saints at Philippi. Tomorrow we will think on the fact that Paul remembered these saints with THANKFULNESS. On Saturday we will see that he prayed for them with JOYFULNESS. And on Sunday we will observe that he appreciated them with GRATEFULNESS. As we spend these few minutes each day examining Paul's teaching, let us purpose anew to realize just how much true Christian friends mean to us. We might ask ourselves sincerely what we think our lives might be were it not for such people.

PRAYER: Dear Father, we thank You for the Christian friends You have brought into our lives. We are grateful especially for those who have had that extra influence on us for God and good. And above all, we praise You for the Friend who sticks closer than a brother, Jesus Christ, who is everything to us. Amen.

## REMEMBERING FRIENDS WITH THANKFULNESS

The warmth of Paul's spirit toward his Christian friends at Philippi is seen in verse 3. He remembers them with an expression of THANKFULNESS. He writes, "I thank my God every time I remember you." Blessed is the man who has such pleasant memories!

Ellicott has said, "It is a lovely thing when remembrance and gratitude are bound up together."[1] That was Paul's experience when he remembered these saints to whom he originally wrote this epistle. Every time memories of these Christians flooded his mind, thankfulness welled up in his heart to God! What recollections do you have of Christians who have been special to you? In the lives of most of us who have come to know Christ, God has used someone (probably more than one) in a unique way to bring us to himself—and we, too, remember them with thankfulness!

In my own background God has used a multitude of people through the years to help me ever and again to appreciate more and more the value of the will of God. But there are seven persons in particular whose combined influence has become a permanent motivating factor in my life. They have helped to shape my heart-life in more concrete and tangible ways—their influence has been more lasting than others.

My respect for them has given them the guarded right, at my permission, to cautiously invade my life—they have offered a special word of advice, sincere encouragement to pray, a challenge to think more carefully and evaluate more thoroughly, a reminder to keep God first, reinforcement to be true to the Bible—and the result has been good. Who are they? They are

---

[1]From *The Letters to the Philippians, Colossians, and Thessalonians* (Revised Edition), translated and interpreted by William Barclay. Copyright © 1975 William Barclay. Published in the U.S.A. by The Westminster Press, p. 13. Used and adapted by permission.

JOY IN A ROMAN JAIL

a mother who loved, a pastor who made Jesus real to me, a high school friend who lived Christ before me, a Bible school professor whose sanctified life challenged me, a college professor who deeply respected the Bible, another pastor who preached Christ with God-given passion, and a wife who has loved me and stood with me when I was at my best and at my worst—all of these have helped to mold and fashion my present attitude toward God and life. And God knows that they all will share in any success in the cause of Christ that I may ever have. I say with Paul, "I thank my God every time I remember them!"

We will do ourselves an eternal favor, on the other hand, while remembering those who have influenced us, to recall that our lives are also influencing others! Periodically we ought to ask ourselves, "What memories will others have of me?" I try to remind my own heart often that there are at least four persons in this world who are forming lasting memories concerning my life. My wife is one. My three children are the others, one of whom has already left our home to establish his own. All four will recall some of my good qualities. And all four will remember some of my less desirable characteristics (I thank God that they have been very patient with me). My sincere prayer is that God will help me to so live that most of their memories will be good!

In our text, the evidence is that these Christians at Philippi had left many good memories which lingered in the thoughts of Paul. "I thank my God every time I remember you." Doubly blessed, that man Paul!

*PRAYER: Great God, and loving heavenly Father, we know that no man lives to himself and none of us dies to himself. We know that today we will cast some type of influence on someone. Fill us anew with the Holy Spirit so that we will be able to make it easy for those whose lives we will touch to believe in You and in Your Son, Jesus Christ. Amen.*

## PRAYING FOR FRIENDS WITH JOYFULNESS

Paul not only remembered his friends at Philippi with THANKFULNESS, but he also prayed for those friends with JOYFULNESS. In verse 4 he writes, "In all my prayers for all of you, I always pray with joy . . ." And there were two reasons why he could afford to pray for them with such joy.

First, he deeply appreciated their partnership in the gospel. Let us pick up verse 5 with verse 4: "In all my prayers for all of you, I always pray with joy *because of your partnership in the gospel* from the first day until now . . ." King James version translates "partnership" with the word "fellowship." Now the question we must consider is this: What is Paul's primary thought when he refers to "partnership (fellowship) in the gospel?" A cramped or warped impression of what this fellowship is may prompt us to be convinced that we have it when we don't, or to imagine we don't have it when we do. Do you suppose that real fellowship is attending the same church? reciting the same creed? repeating the same kind of prayers? socializing with the same group of people? enjoying the same type of worship? agreeing with each other's personal convictions? Is this what fellowship is?

Genuine fellowship primarily involves the entering into a volitional "partnership" centered in propagating *the gospel of Christ*. And we might add that this partnership can be very real whether we attend the same church or not, or recite the same creed or not. Take a doctor and a construction riveter, whose backgrounds and interests are as far apart as those of an artist and a scuba diver—let them find the same Christ and come to love Him deeply. There will be fellowship! How can this be? Because they both have entered into this very real partnership whose over-riding enthusiasm is not found in their "social sameness," but *in the gospel!* The gospel has become their great bond of unity! Because such a fellowship had come to exist between Paul and the Christians at Philippi, he says that when he prays for them it is with joy!

The second reason that Paul could afford to pray for them with joy was because of his confidence in God's power to complete the work He had begun in them. Look at verse 6: "Being confident of this, that He who began a good work in you will carry it on to completion until the day of Christ Jesus." Note carefully how Paul's eye is on "the day of Christ Jesus"— the future.

When these saints at Philippi first became believers, God "began a good work in their hearts" as He has done in the hearts of all in every generation who have repented and believed. Paul emphasizes this fact in our context: "He . . . *began* a good work in you."

In one sense, of course, the work God effects in the heart of one who believes is complete. He is completely saved! He is totally forgiven! The Holy Spirit makes him an entirely new creation on the inside. This is a complete work of God's grace!

Ah, but following that complete conversion, the Holy Spirit *continues* to work in the believer's heart and life, teaching, guiding, disciplining, purging, knocking off the rough edges, leading to deeper commitment and to consecration! What is God doing? He is *bringing to completion* "that good work" which He began in his heart at conversion! And that work will finally be culminated when the rapture introduces "the day of Christ Jesus" and he inherits a glorified body! The lapel badge being worn by so many Christians, on which are the letters "PBPGINFWMY," says it all. The letters mean, "Please be patient —God is not finished with me yet!" How true!

We Christians are so prone to become blinded by another's imperfections that we question his sincerity and commitment. We tend to forget that others also see our own imperfections and might well question our sincerity and commitment. H.A. Ironside used to tell of an artist who had conceived in his mind a great picture which he meant to become a masterpiece. He was working on a large canvas, putting in dabs of gray which would become background. A friend entered and watched his work. Turning, the artist asked, "What do you think of this? I intend it to become the greatest work I have ever done!" His friend laughed, "To be quite frank . . . it seems to me to be only a great dab." "Oh," replied the artist, "but you cannot see what is going to be there—I can!"[1] And there is the difference! God is able to see in us all that which will emerge at the judgment seat of Christ. And He keeps on working to "carry it on to completion until the day of Christ Jesus."

Here is the lesson—as fellow Christians, we must continually endeavor to see past each other's shortcomings and failures, and "be confident" that God will finish His work in both of us! Such an attitude, if deeply sincere, will greatly enhance our spiritual relationships with each other. We, too, will be able to say, "In all my prayers for all of you, I always pray with joy!"

*PRAYER: Loving Lord, grant that this which we call "fellowship" with our Christian friends will truly be "in the gospel." Help us to volitionally look at our fellow Christians through the eyes of Jesus. We thank You that You are not finished with any of us yet. Continue to mold us after Your likeness, that You may bring to completion Your good work in us until the day of Jesus Christ, in whose name we pray. Amen.*

---

[1]From *Philippians* by H.A. Ironside. Copyright © 1978 by Loizeaux Brothers, pp. 19-20. Used by permission.

WEEK 2: *Sunday*
READ: *Philippians 1:3-8 one final time (note especially today verses 7-8)*

## APPRECIATING FRIENDS WITH GRATEFULNESS

On Friday we saw that Paul remembered his friends in Christ who were at Philippi with THANKFULNESS. Yesterday we thought on the fact that he prayed for those friends with JOY-FULNESS. Today we note that he appreciated them with GRATEFULNESS. "It is right for me to feel this way about all of you, since I have you in my heart," he writes, "for whether I am in chains or defending and confirming the gospel, all of you share in God's grace with me." Apparently when Paul was placed in chains in prison (he was confined in jail at the time of this writing), some at Philippi had been willing on various occasions to be so identified with him that either they were threatened with prison themselves, or they had actually been incarcerated. When Paul had been thrown into controversy with religionists and forced to tenaciously defend the gospel, these believers demonstrated their total allegiance to his cause.

One of the identifying characteristics of the Christians of Paul's day was that they loved each other! And they person-alized that love by being willing to stand with each other in the time of trouble. The writer of Hebrews, in chapter 10, alludes to this fierce loyalty these believers had for each other: "Re-member those earlier days after you had received the light, when you stood your ground in a great contest in the face of suffering. Sometimes you stood side by side with those who were so treated. You sympathized with those in prison and joyfully accepted the confiscation of your property, because you knew that you your-selves had better and lasting possessions" (Hebrews 10:32-34). This is precisely what these at Philippi had done when Paul was placed in prison for preaching the gospel—they "stood side by side" with him!

In our country of the United States, Christians seem to be

overly geared to "independency" and "denominationalism." We are not extremely blessed with such fiber so necessary to "stand together" during times of trouble or misunderstanding. While serving as missionaries in the country of Nigeria, my wife and I observed groups of the evangelical church faithfully standing side by side with each other. They loyally defended each other during times of pressure from Moslem leaders or pagan chiefs. That is not to say that they never argued theology or questioned each other's practices—but they stood together! They had to! The pagans did. The Moslems did. And the evangelical Christians chose to do the same! When one suffered, fellow Christians did not question whether he was of the Baptists, or the Evangelical Church of Africa, or the Sudan United Mission, or the United Missionary Society. If he was a born again Christian, they stood with him!

What does this mean to us in our society? It means quite practically, for instance, that when either a Jerry Falwell or a Jim Bakker is criticized for his effort to stem society's blatant attempt to force public acceptance of the homosexual lifestyle, that we stand with him. You may retort, "But I am not a Baptist and neither am I a charismatic!" No one would ask you, at this point, to be a Baptist or a charismatic! That is not the issue! The fact is, the cause is right and in harmony with the gospel! When Christians take a stand against the right of "abortion on demand" in our country, though we may not choose to carry a placard or join a march, we will stand for such a cause, for it is right and scriptural! We must stand side by side!

That is what the Philippian Christians did with Paul, who seemed to be so gifted at landing in jail. They themselves were able to stay out of prison—at least the majority were never arrested for the gospel's sake. But they did not go around criticizing Paul for his boldness that resulted in his imprisonment on numerous occasions. They stood with him! They supported him! As a result, Paul says in verse 8, "God can testify how I long for all of you with the affection of Christ Jesus." So be it today!

*PRAYER: Dear Father, help us not to be critical of our brothers and sisters in Christ. Help us to stand with each other in prayer, and to encourage each other in Christ. Thank you for those who have believed in us in spite of our weaknesses. Help us today to be able to return that attitude to someone else, for Christ's sake. Amen.*

## PRAYING FOR FELLOW CHRISTIANS (1:9-11)

**Pray for Our Love to be Multiplied (1:9)**
**Pray for Our Leading to be Clarified (1:9)**
**Pray for Our Label to be Bona Fide (1:10)**
**Pray for Our Lives to be Justified (1:11)**

WEEK 2:  Monday
READ:  Philippians 1:9-11

## PRAYING FOR FELLOW CHRISTIANS

A thread-bare statement exchanged often among Christians goes like this: "I'll be remembering you in prayer." Do we, in fact, really fulfill that pledge which we so thoughtlessly offer at times to others? More precisely, what are our primary considerations when we pray for God's saints—especially those who seem to be so consistently victorious, who seldom appear to be anything else but "on top" of their circumstances and invariably healthy?

The type of people for whom Paul is praying in our text most definitely graced this description. They were expressing Christ so well that Paul could say to them, "I thank my God every time I remember you." Howbeit, they still needed prayer— and it is evident that Paul prayed for them often. In our text, he gives an example of the kind of prayers he offered to God on their behalf. And in this simple prayer he reveals what were his deep concerns for these victorious, joyful people!

Let us learn a lesson! Matter it not how deeply dedicated one may be to Christ, or how triumphant in his faith, he will never ascend to the spiritual plain where he will have no more needs necessitating prayer help from fellow Christians! We are all needy people! And that fact ought to motivate us to pray for each other often!

Paul alludes to some of these needs in this section. For the next four days we will examine rather carefully four definite needs that characterize "on top" Christians which ought to prompt us to be very faithful in our prayers for each other. If it appears to you that we will be spending an abundance of time considering a very small parcel of the Word of God, please be patient. It is a very important segment concerning prayer. And I have discovered through the years that, if God's people are ever to be faulted for being over-zealous, it is not at the point of praying too much! So let us consider these four needs, one each day for the next four days and profit thereby. Paul prays in this section that: OUR LOVE BE MULTIPLIED, OUR LEADING BE CLARIFIED, OUR LABEL BE BONA FIDE, OUR LIVES BE JUSTIFIED. And as we study, let us pledge ourselves to pray more often and more sincerely for our fellow brothers and sisters in Christ.

PRAYER: *Wonderful Savior, we thank You for the exam-*

*ple that You set in prayer recorded for us in the New Testament. You prayed for Your followers, and we are very much aware that we, Your present day disciples, need to pray for each other. Help us to do so out of love for them and for You. Amen.*

———————————•—•—•——————————

*WEEK 2:  Tuesday*
*READ: Philippians 1:9-11 again (focus attention on verse 9)*

## PRAY FOR OUR LOVE TO BE MULTIPLIED

In his prayer Paul clarifies that, as true Christians, we need OUR LOVE TO BE MULTIPLIED. Look at verse 9 where he says, "And this is my prayer: that your love may abound more and more . . ." Stop there. We should be reminded that the word he uses here is "agape." He is not referring to social, brotherly love or to the love between a husband and wife. Other words express those types of love. This is filial love—and is the same word used when John, in his first epistle, declared, "God is love." It is invariably the word used when the New Testament writers refer to God's love being implanted in our hearts by the Holy Spirit.

The cut of love depicted in our text cannot be "coerced into existence" by the simple manipulation of human volition. It cannot be trumped up! We must become *recipients* of this brand of love through the incoming of the Holy Spirit in His regenerating power! Jesus, in His response to a lawyer's question concerning which was the most important commandment of all, stated that the exercise of "agape" love was more important than fulfilling any of the other commandments. Here are his words: " 'Love the Lord your God with all your heart, with all your soul, with all your mind and with all your strength.' The second is this: 'Love your neighbor as yourself.' There is no greater commandment than these. All the Law and the Prophets hang on these two commandments." (Matthew 22:34-39; Mark 12:28-31).

Now, Paul's drive in our text is not simply that we come to embrace this love in our hearts. His greatest thrust is, "that your love may abound more and more"! Toward whom? Toward God first, of course. And beyond that, toward our fellow saints. In our context he speaks more to the practical aspect of love's attitudes between Christians. His overriding concern is that our God-given love *for each other* will grow and increase more and more!

So the question which makes this thought workable is this: How can you and I allow God to multiply His love in our hearts so that, in a practical way, we will love Him more and more, and love His people more and more? At the risk of bordering on oversimplification, let me dare to streamline a Biblical response: "To receive more of such love, receive more of the Holy Spirit!" We must sincerely wait upon God in prayer and complete consecration and, by faith, allow the Holy Spirit to possess us fully. And as we continue to maintain an attitude of total yieldedness to Him, He will increasingly pour His love into our hearts and slowly intensify our ability to manifest that love in down to earth ways which will make our practical effectiveness as Christians more evident. At this point we all need God's help! So let us ask Him often.

*PRAYER: Author of divine love, fill our hearts anew with the Holy Spirit that the love which He gives will ever be increasing in us. Teach us how to properly manifest that love both to You and to others. Thank you for the power of the Spirit who enables us to so love. Help us to evidence that love in a very workable way today. Amen.*

WEEK 2: *Wednesday*
READ: *Philippians 1:9-11 (again focus attention on verse 9)*

### PRAY FOR OUR LEADING TO BE CLARIFIED

In his prayer for the saints at Philippi and for Christians of all ages, Paul clarifies that, not only ought OUR LOVE TO BE MULTIPLIED, as we observed in yesterday's study, but OUR LEADING OUGHT TO BE CLARIFIED. Refer again to verse 9: "And this is my prayer: that your love may abound more and more *in knowledge and depth of insight."* The King James Version translates that last phrase, "in knowledge and in all judgment." If we are to be truly scriptural in the manifestation of God's love in our everyday lives, then we must keep certain, as Paul Rees used to put it, "that there is no rift between the enkindled heart and the enlightened mind."[1]

Born again people can be very naive! The sincere deacon was honest, but sadly wrong, when he declared to his Bible class, "If God's love is in our *hearts*, it really doesn't matter how much we understand in our minds—it is the heart that counts, not the head!" Such an over-simplified philosophy overlooks one very important issue. Unless the mind be sufficiently enlightened, a zealous heart can drive a very sincere person to perform some foolish and spiritually damaging actions!

A very striking example emerges in the Gospels. Jesus healed a leper. Mark tells us that He instructed the man not to tell anyone what had happened. But the man was thrilled and grateful for the healing, and ignoring what Jesus had said, "went out and began to talk freely, spreading the news. As a result, Jesus

---

[1]From *The Adequate Man* by Paul S. Rees. Copyright © 1959 by Fleming H. Revell Company, pp. 21-22. Used by permission.

could no longer enter a town openly . . ." (Mark 1:40-45). You see, his heart was warm and his motive right—but his timing was pathetically wrong! His heart was enkindled, but his mind was not enlightened. And his actions did more harm to the ministry of Jesus, at this stage, than good. Jesus could not enter openly into any surrounding city as a result. This recipient of Christ's healing needed his love to abound more and more *"in knowledge"!*

Now from whence does this "knowledge" and "depth of insight" come? They must come through an ever-increasing understanding of the Word of God, the Bible! Let us realize unmistakably that there is no overly simplified way to receive divine "knowledge" and "depth of insight" apart from a consistent and careful study of God's holy Word! Life is full of circumstances which demand decisions on our part. Having the love of God infused into our hearts does not automatically render the implications of those decisions easier to understand. It is not always easy to recognize what the will of God is under some circumstances. We must be able to comprehend some of the cardinal principles of the teaching of the Scriptures. We must come to understand how those principles apply to our present day and society. Some type of personal in-depth study of the Bible (much more than a "reading-the-Bible-through-in-a-year" type of thing) is absolutely necessary if those Biblical fundamentals are to be sufficiently transposed to our surroundings. Through such careful study, God's Spirit can give us adequate guidance that is truly safe and scriptural when applied to the unique circumstances of our varied lives!

I became involved in a rather lengthy discussion with a sincere Christian some months ago. His candid opinion was that God could and would guide him just as unmistakably by the "inner voice of the Spirit" as He could and would by His written Word. I had no argument with the fact that God can guide an individual by His Holy Spirit or by what my friend would call "the inner light." But I took strong exception to the proposition which would ascribe to *that type* of guidance the same level of authority as recognized in God's written Word, the Bible. Such guidance, by its very nature, is extremely subjective and must be sifted through a maze of very human emotions—and therein lies the danger! Human as we are, we are ever prone to act upon "what we feel on the inside" as opposed to acting upon the authority of solid principles which have become clear to us as a result of hard study of the Word of God.

Let our "knowledge" and "depth of insight" come from the one *sure Word of Prophecy*, the Bible! And why do we need such "knowledge" and "depth of insight"? The apostle speaks to that point in his prayer: "And this is my prayer: that your love may abound more and more in knowledge and depth of insight, *so that you may be able to discern what is best.*" To be able to so "discern what is best" is not always easy—but with an ever-enlarging knowledge of the Word of God, a solid foundation is laid for true guidance from the Author of the authoritative Word. God, grant us such direction!

*PRAYER: Dear Father, You know how prone we can be to make lasting decisions based upon shallow emotional reactions to circumstances in which we find ourselves. Help us to take the time to carefully study Your Word, purposing to live by its principles. Through that Word, give us "knowledge" and "depth of insight" so that we may live our lives that Christ will truly be glorified. Amen.*

*READ: Philippians 1:9-11 (center attention on verse 10 today)*

## PRAY FOR OUR LABEL TO BE BONA FIDE

Tuesday we learned that we need OUR LOVE TO BE MULTIPLIED, and yesterday we came to realize that OUR LEADING MUST BE CLARIFIED. Today the thought that will take our attention is this: OUR LABEL MUST BE BONA FIDE. In verse 10 we read in Paul's prayer that our love may abound more and more in knowledge and depth of insight, so that we ". . . may be pure and blameless until the day of Christ." I like the King James rendering of this phrase: ". . . that ye may be sincere and without offense till the day of Christ." Paul's mind at this point in his prayer is focused upon the idea of "genuineness" or "being for real."

The English word "sincere" is from the Latin term "sincerus," thought by some to be derived from two other Latin expressions. The one is "sine" which means "without." The second is "cera" which means "wax." So, according to these scholars, the English word "sincere" originally meant quite literally "without wax."[1] A few years ago we purchased a new stereo. When delivered, it had a small chip on the lid. We contacted the company and a representative came to our home. He explained that one of two things could be done. Either the company would pay for a new lid straight out, or else he would fix it to "look as good as new." We chose the second. With a small stick of wax of the same shade as the lid he filled the chipped area, squared it off and shined it. Today our stereo appears to be perfect. However, the truth remains. It is not quite what it appears to be. It is "with wax." A part of it is not real.

In ancient days dealers in porcelain performed the same operation on pieces of pottery which had become cracked while being fired. The dealer, filling the flaw with wax, would

---

[1]The origin of the Latin word "sincerus" is questionable. Some scholars have felt the word is formed from "sine" and "cera." The majority of dictionaries, however, would hold that it comes from "sine" and a word akin to "caries"—literally, "without decay."

smooth it until it appeared to be perfect. But a buyer could hold the piece of porcelain up to the light and the light would reveal the wax! An honest dealer would refer to a piece which had no wax added as being "sine cera"—without wax. It was truly what it appeared to be. That is the drive of the word Paul utilizes here. We ought to strive to be "real people" genuine and pure, without wax. When held up to the light of the Word of God, we will be found to be without anything that is false in our profession!

Further, he prays that we not only be genuine, but also "blameless until the day of Christ." His meaning is basically that we be "inoffensive" and "clear of conscience." We can hardly assume correctly that Paul is praying here that true believers will never do anything that would prompt other people to feel they have a right to "blame them" or "find fault" with them. That is a type of perfection none of us will ever enjoy in this life! The Bible does, however, promise us enough available grace that we may possess right motives and clear consciences in what we are and do. We may certainly be honest and genuine in our profession of faith in Christ. If I understand verses 9 and 10 correctly, Paul intimates that if we have allowed the Holy Spirit to fill our hearts with the love of God, and if that love is growing—and if we study the Scriptures carefully and endeavor to manifest that love in our lives according to scriptural principles with a genuine profession of faith and a clear conscience —God fully accepts. But remember, He accepts all of our feeble efforts to please Him only in and through Christ! This is what I understand Paul to envision when he prays for the Christians at Philippi and for us to be "pure and blameless (sincere and without offense) until the day of Christ."

PRAYER: *Lord of grace and mercy, help us to be truly sincere and without offense today, and until the day of Christ. Grant us grace to be genuine people, up front and honest, that our testimonies and professions to unsaved friends will be valid and credible. We ask this sincerely for Jesus' sake. Amen.*

## PRAY FOR OUR LIVES TO BE JUSTIFIED

For the past three days, we have been considering the fact that God's people, victorious though they may be, possess particular needs. The recognition of these needs ought to motivate us to be faithful to each other in sincere prayer. We have considered three of these needs thus far. We need OUR LOVE TO BE MULTIPLIED, OUR LEADING TO BE CLARIFIED and OUR LABEL TO BE BONA FIDE. In today's text we will give attention to one final thought from this prayer: we need OUR LIVES TO JUSTIFIED. Look at verse 11. Paul prays that we be "filled with the fruit of righteousness that comes through Jesus Christ—to the glory and praise of God."

When I speak of our lives being justified at this juncture, I am not referring to the justification which is embraced by faith when a sinner trusts Christ as his Savior. That is justification "in the sight of God." The final statement of Paul's prayer in our text involves a type of justification which is "in the sight of people"—justification which is proven by works. You see, the only way any of us can be "justified before people" in our claim that we are "justified before God by faith" is when our works (which people can observe) demonstrate that our profession of faith in Christ is genuine. "The fruit of righteousness" in one's every day life becomes the confirmation of "inner righteousness" in his heart. Jesus said, "By their fruit you will recognize them" (Matthew 7:16).

Now we must understand clearly—Paul asserts that this is "the fruit of righteousness *that comes through Jesus Christ,*" and is *"to the glory and praise of God!"* This does not even hint to the thought of "self righteousness" legally performed void of Christ in the heart. Only God knows how many have never given their hearts to the Lord Jesus, but who have set out to "prove to others how good they are" by "the performance of good and noble deeds" and by "refraining from numerous evil practices." How different are those who have allowed Christ to invade their hearts; who then, out of true love for their Savior, live out lives which produce "good fruit." That is the focal point of Paul's statement in today's Scripture lesson. Let us learn thereby and so be "filled with the fruit of righteousness that comes through Jesus Christ—to the glory and praise of God."

PRAYER: *Father of righteousness, we commit ourselves anew to You today, asking that You will give us the needed grace to allow the righteousness of Christ to be lived out through us to the glory of God. We praise You for the Holy Spirit who lives in us as the Divine Enabler, the Holy Empowerer, to manifest such righteousness. May we draw on His power to so live today. Amen.*

┌─────────────────────────────────────────────┐

## THE VALUE OF UNWELCOME
## CIRCUMSTANCES (1:12-19)

**Spiritual Enlightenment for Sinners (1:12-13)**
**Spiritual Encouragement for the Saved (1:14-18)**
**Spiritual Enablement for the Subject (1:19)**

└─────────────────────────────────────────────┘

*WEEK 2: Saturday*
*READ: Philippians 1:12-19*

## THE VALUE OF UNWELCOME CIRCUMSTANCES

A friend of Dr. Lloyd Ogilvie, senior pastor of the First Pres-
byterian Church in Hollywood, California, asked him rather
unexpectedly one day, "Lloyd, tell me, what's one of the most
crucial discoveries you have made in the past ten years?" Dr.
Ogilvie said, "I looked at the intense expression on my friend's
face [and realized] . . . he was not putting me on . . . My answer
came quickly, distilled by years of joy and pain, 'Everything
that happens to us is for what God wants to have happen to us;
everything that happens to us is for what God wants to have
happen to others, through us.'"[1]

We take one of our greatest steps toward true victorious living
when we learn to trust God *with* and *in* our circumstances—
especially the unwelcome circumstances! More times than not,
it is through these circumstances that God desires to reveal himself to us in ways never before realized. And through us He
wants to manifest himself to others! Yet, how often we must
confess that when we find ourselves under pressure, provocation
or what we might consider to be persecution, our reaction to

---

[1]From *Let God Love You* by Lloyd John Ogilvie. Copyright © 1978 by Word Books,
p. 30. Used by permission.

such sudden unexpected conditions exposes a weakness in our make-up which causes us embarrassment and shame.

Our attitudes toward the restrictions of such unwelcome circumstances will, without doubt, determine our depth of spiritual development and progress. In fact, our attitudes under such stress and strain will probably either "make or break" us spiritually!

Paul faced such a circumstance. He alludes to it in the text for today. For years his burden to journey to Rome to preach the gospel had almost become an obsession. He had written in his letter to the Christians at Rome, "I am ready to preach the gospel to you that are at Rome also" (Romans 1:15). In Acts he said, "I must also see Rome" (Acts 19:21). Little did he realize the conditions under which he would finally make that journey! When he finally saw the capital city of the empire, he arrived in chains, not as a preacher, but as a prisoner! He had been hauled to trial for preaching Christ in his own country and, recognizing that he would receive no justice there, had appealed to Caesar, which every Roman citizen had the right to do. He traveled to Rome under military escort—and Rome paid his passage! There he was handed over to the "captain of the guard." Eventually he was allowed to dwell in his own hired house, but always under military guard—apparently chained to a Roman soldier most of the time.

So here was Paul—waiting, praying, hoping to be able to preach the gospel at Rome! And he finally got there—but under arrest and chained! Weren't those a set of exciting circumstances? They were unwelcome circumstances to say the least. From his prison, then, he penned the lines of this epistle.

Over the next three days we will observe how God used this unwelcome circumstance to reveal himself to Paul and, through Paul, to others. On Sunday we will see how God used Paul's unwelcome circumstance to bring SPIRITUAL ENLIGHTEN-MENT TO SINNERS. On Monday we will observe how he used those circumstances for the SPIRITUAL ENCOURAGE-MENT OF THE SAVED, and on Tuesday, for the SPIRITUAL

ENABLEMENT OF THE SUBJECT. As we study, let us be good learners!

*PRAYER: O God of all our circumstances, we confess that we do not always demonstrate a good spirit under some unwelcome occasions. Grant Your forgiveness. Help us to learn that You do not permit anything to enter our lives or cross our paths except that, through that circumstance, You want to teach us something for our good—or else teach someone else something for their good through us. Please help us not to frustrate that plan through a disgruntled or bitter spirit. We pray this in Jesus' name with thanksgiving. Amen.*

*WEEK 3: Sunday*
*READ: Philippians 1:12-19 (look at verses 12-13)*

### SPIRITUAL ENLIGHTENMENT FOR SINNERS
### (THROUGH UNWELCOME CIRCUMSTANCES)

When Paul journeyed to Rome as a prisoner of the government, the circumstance under which he found himself was not what he had hoped for and certainly not what he would have welcomed. But God employed that unwelcome circumstance to accomplish good! For one thing, He utilized it for the SPIRITUAL ENLIGHTENMENT OF SINNERS. In verse 12 we read, "'Now I want you to know, brothers, that what has happened to me has really served to advance the gospel." He could have deplored his imprisonment as an interruption to his preaching of the gospel. Instead he allowed God to use this imprisonment to "advance the gospel." His deepest concern was this: "How can God use what has happened to me for the progress of the good news of Christ?"

Now get the picture. Here is Paul, for two years waiting to go to trial. He is allowed to rent his own house, but is constantly chained to a Roman guard. The guards are changed periodically —but there is always one there. Is he to accept this as a hindrance to preaching? Not Paul! He had a ready-made congregation of one all the time! And there was no way he could get up and walk out on Paul's sermon! Not only was Paul chained to him—he was also chained to Paul! Do you have any doubts that Paul would preach to these burly men of the military? I don't.

Time passed. Eventually visitors were allowed to come and speak with the prisoner. Paul, and they, too, spoke of Christ— the Roman guards heard it all. We read in the last two verses of Acts, "For two whole years Paul stayed there in his own rented house and welcomed all who came to see him. Boldly and without hindrance he preached the kingdom of God and taught about the Lord Jesus Christ" (Acts 28:30-31). Since the guards were changed continually, many of them heard the message of Christ! And apparently some of these soldiers were converted and began to witness to what they had come to believe and experience. By the time Paul wrote this epistle, he could say in verse 13, "As a result, it has become clear throughout the whole palace guard and to everyone else that I am in chains for Christ." Not only so, but the influence of the gospel had affected the very household of Caesar. Possibly some of these had believed before Paul arrived, but very likely some were inspired to believe in Christ through Paul's witness (note 4:22).

What are some of your unwelcome circumstances? Satan is intent on making you feel that so long as these persist, you cannot be an effective witness for the Lord Jesus. Not true! God can transform those unwelcome incidents into stepping stones!

Many have read the books by Joni Eareckson Tada. Injured in a diving accident and paralyzed from the shoulders down, it appeared to be the end of the world for a 17-year-old girl who had a zest for life. But rather than buckle under the devastating disappointment of that incident, she has allowed God to transpose seeming tragedy and its results into an open opportunity to bear effective witness for Christ. She has dictated two books, paints religious cards and posters by holding the pen in her mouth, has portrayed herself in two feature films, and the world has heard of her and of her Christ! What has happened to her has really served "to advance the gospel."

The fact is, God's purpose is to use every circumstance which He allows to enter our lives to work into our hearts a deeper desire and ability to be a more effective sharer of His grace. And that He will do—unless we block the ministry of His Spirit by becoming bitter or disenchanted as a result of that circumstance.

In Paul's case, God used his unwelcome circumstance for the SPIRITUAL ENLIGHTENMENT OF THE SINNERS among the Roman guards assigned to keep him imprisoned and among many in Caesar's very household. Will we allow Him to use the unwelcome circumstances of our lives to "advance the gospel" as well?

*PRAYER: Christ of the living God, breathe into us the grace we need to know how to allow You to use what happens to us to really serve to advance the gospel. We know that this will not happen automatically, so grant us the power of Your Holy Spirit to enable us to act positively upon such knowledge, we pray in the name of our Savior. Amen.*

WEEK 3: *Monday*
READ: *Philippians 1:12-19 (read again verses 14-18)*

## SPIRITUAL ENCOURAGEMENT FOR THE SAVED
## (THROUGH UNWELCOME CIRCUMSTANCES)

Not only did Paul use his unwelcome circumstance for the SPIRITUAL ENLIGHTENMENT OF SINNERS, as we saw yesterday, but he also made the best of his situation in order to bring about the SPIRITUAL ENCOURAGEMENT OF THE SAVED. Notice verse 14 carefully: "Because of my chains, most of the brothers in the Lord have been encouraged to speak the word of God more courageously and fearlessly." Apparently the Roman authorities had succeeded in frightening a good number of the Christians in that city into silence. They were exercising no effective witness for Christ at all—their courage was nil. They were "secret disciples." But when they received the news that Paul was bearing witness for Christ though chained as a prisoner, they became much emboldened to "come out in the open" with their witness! And when they heard that some of Paul's guards had been converted to Christ, they, too, began to speak the Word of God fearlessly! Maybe you have been intimidated into silence by the attitudes and actions of ungodly people with whom you work. Do you need someone to give you encouragement? On the other hand, could it be that others with whom you work are Christians, but are not very strong in the Lord? Do they need someone to give them encouragement? By the power of the indwelling Spirit, you ought to be the one to give them that needed strength by your own effective witness for Christ! God help you to become such!

Some of those who were empowered by Paul's fearless spirit began to bear testimony for Christ with a pure motive of love "out of good will." Others, sadly, for whatever reason, took advantage of Paul's imprisonment to capitalize on his courage and also began to witness—but not sincerely. They commenced to "preach Christ out of selfish ambition, not sincerely." Paul says in verse 15 that "envy and rivalry" motivated these, and in verse 17, they supposed they could stir up trouble for him while he was in chains. Just why they were so intent to embarrass Paul and his ministry is not made clear. I think it is relatively safe to assume that they were in disagreement with either some facet of truth which he taught or with some of the methods he had used to propagate the gospel. Maybe both!

The real issue is not to discover why these misled brethren had reacted so to the ministry of Paul. The real point to note carefully is how Paul reacted to them! His attitude is disarming. Look at what he says in verse 18: "But what does it matter? The important thing is that in every way, whether from false motives or true, Christ is preached. And because of this I rejoice." Paul did not condone their wrong motives nor their spirit of envy and rivalry. But his *greatest* concern was that the gospel of Christ be preached! He knew that, though God would not honor wrong motives, He would honor His Word! And therein he rejoiced.

Let us take a lesson! The issue of concern to us ought not to be whether others totally agree with everything we say and believe, or whether or not they are in harmony with our peculiar methods. The point of attention must be "that in every way . . . Christ is preached!" Through the centuries God has, of necessity, overruled many less than perfect attitudes on the part of numerous propagators of the gospel. He has chosen to bless His Word in spite of some of the foolish methods utilized by His servants. He has ushered repentant believing sinners into the kingdom of Christ in spite of misrepresentations of certain doctrinal truths. He has blessed good motives and has blessed in spite of wrong motives! And so shall it ever be so long as He chooses to use human instruments to disperse His message!

The overriding lesson in today's text, however, is one of great importance to you and me. Let us keep a strict and careful guard on our own motives and attitudes as we bear our witness for Christ! Let us ever strive to be among those who radiate Christ "out of good will"—and let us always do so "in love."

*PRAYER: Thou examiner of our thoughts and motives, fill us anew with the Holy Spirit today that our sharing of Christ will truly be out of good will and prompted by God-given love both for You and for others. Grant that in any unwelcome circumstance we may face we will be able to encourage ourselves and others to a more effective and courageous witness for You. Amen.*

————————•—•—•————————

*WEEK 3: Tuesday*
*READ: Philippians 1:12-19 (take note of verse 19)*

## SPIRITUAL ENABLEMENT FOR THE SUBJECT (THROUGH UNWELCOME CIRCUMSTANCES)

We have seen in our study these past two days how God used the unwelcome circumstance in the life of Paul to bring SPIRITUAL ENLIGHTENMENT TO SINNERS and SPIRITUAL ENCOURAGEMENT TO THE SAVED. Today we want to consider how He used this undesirable occasion to bring SPIRITUAL ENABLEMENT TO THE SUBJECT, i.e. to Paul himself. Let us read verse 19: "Yes, and I will continue to rejoice, for I know that through your prayers and the help given by the Spirit of Jesus Christ, what has happened to me will turn out for my deliverance."

A surface reading of the New Testament account of the life and ministry of the Apostle Paul and a shallow study of his epistles might tempt us to conclude that he was always "on top" of all his unwelcome circumstances. We might reason that, since he and Silas were able to sing the night away while in jail in Philippi, *all* of his prison experiences became "settings for song-time." That is hardly the case. During his two-year imprisonment in Rome (from where he wrote this epistle), it is clearly apparent that at times he was not certain whether he would live or die. He wondered *how* he would survive this prison experience and, at times, wondered *if* he would come through at all. But two things gave Paul much confidence that what had happened to him would turn out for his deliverance (whether deliverance from prison or deliverance into the presence of Christ): first, the prayers of the saints at Philippi, and second, the help given by the Holy Spirit!

Take that first thought—the prayers of his fellow Christians. Some of God's choicest people have been called upon to face unbearable circumstances, and have exhausted themselves trying to understand the "why's." Were it not for the fact that they knew others of their brothers and sisters in Christ were sincerely praying for them, they would not have survived spiritually or emotionally.

My wife and I sat in the living room of an acquaintance six years ago. We were sharing with a lovely Christian lady who had lost her husband in death so completely unexpectedly. He had been the victim of a brain hemorrhage at a time in life when they could have just begun to enjoy together some of the joys of having successfully raised their family. They had wanted to travel a little, and "just do some of the things together that they had not been able to do previously." Now her husband was gone. The trauma of his untimely death drove her to the brink of complete despair. Deep depression engulfed her. She prayed until she was prayed out! She wept until she was totally exhausted. God seemed so far away and so unreal that her further attempts to talk to Him only seemed to mock her. She counseled with her pastor, desperately trying to grasp something that would help her survive spiritually and emotionally. Her spiritually sensitive and godly shepherd gave her the best advice she could have received at that point in her life. He said to her, "I don't want you to try to pray anymore! We of the congregation will pray for you! You let us pray—we'll carry your load for you the best we can." She told my wife and me, "I did just that!" And it worked! Not overnight, but over a period of time and with further counseling—and with her fellow Christians praying—she was able to find the peace necessary for spiritual and emotional stability. She not only survived, but stands today as living witness that "through (their) prayers . . . what (had happened to her turned) out for (her) deliverance." Oh how we all need the prayers of one another! Let us never become weary in fulfilling such a ministry!

What else gave Paul confidence? The help given by the Spirit of Jesus Christ! And after all, here is our true source of victory and deliverance! If for no other reason, here is motive enough for every Christian to seek to be filled with the Holy Spirit. Through His indwelling presence and power, God will help us to use our unwelcome circumstances for our own SPIRITUAL ENABLEMENT.

PRAYER: *Dear heavenly Father, we thank You for every Christian who takes time to pray sincerely for us. We thank You for Your Holy Spirit who dwells in our unworthy hearts. Help us to be faithful in the ministry of prayer on behalf of our brothers and sisters in the Lord, especially those who are facing very unwelcome circumstances in their lives. Grant that those circumstances, through our prayers and through the help given by the Spirit of Jesus Christ, will turn out for their deliverance. We ask this in Jesus' name. Amen.*

### THOUGHTS ON LIFE AND DEATH (1:20-26)

Paul's Attitude Toward Life or Death (1:20)
Paul's Assessment of Life and Death (1:21)
Paul's Alternative Between Life and Death (1:22-26)

*WEEK 3: Wednesday*
*READ: Philippians 1:20-26*

## THOUGHTS ON LIFE AND DEATH

Periodically every one of us ought to push aside all speculations of lesser importance and conduct a thorough evaluation of our innermost thoughts concerning the life we are living and the death we will die. We need to ask ourselves at least two very personal questions concerning our lives. First, just what do we believe is the most important ingredient in life—more important than anything else? Second, do our lives truly *demonstrate* that what we *profess* is important *is, in fact,* that important to us?

We ought to ask ourselves at least four very personal questions about dying. First, with what attitude do we expect to die? Second, what do we really believe is involved in dying? Third, what do we believe lies beyond death for us? And fourth, are we really inculcating into our lives those elements necessary to adequately prepare us for what we say we believe about death?

The writer of this Philippian epistle possessed ample reason to ask himself all of these questions and more. His life had been under threat more than once. Actual attempts had been made to kill him. He lived in the shadow of death so often that in 1 Corinthians 15:31 he recorded, "I die every day." Even as he penned this letter, he was a prisoner of the Roman government

—a government which had all the power necessary to have him executed for his beliefs in Jesus Christ. During his long waiting period under guard (at least two years), Paul had much time to carefully assess what life meant to him, and what death would mean to him. And, at this point in his ministry, he could afford to take time to appraise which of the two would be best for him and which would be most profitable for his fellow saints in Christ.

The world is full of those who expend their entire lives refusing to come to terms with the fact that someday they will die. Their attitudes are entirely negative. They fear dying. To outrun death is their greatest challenge in life.

Others are different. Their greatest problems do not center in death and dying. Their greatest concern is that they have never learned how to truly live! Life to them is meaningless. Like George Bernard Shaw, they must assert, "Life is a disease!"

Paul maintains in our text that, to the born again Christian, both life and death can be full of meaning. Life can exceed just being alive, and death can be more than simply ceasing to live. Life can be worth every bit of all of the living involved, and death can be "gain"! For the next three days we will confine our study to these seven verses (1:20-26), wherein Paul expresses some of his inner thoughts involving his own life and the pressing possibility of his death. Tomorrow we will examine PAUL'S ATTITUDE TOWARD LIFE OR DEATH. On Friday we will see PAUL'S ASSESSMENT OF LIFE AND DEATH, and on Saturday PAUL'S ALTERNATIVE BETWEEN LIFE AND DEATH. As we contemplate his thoughts, let us re-evaluate our own inner reflections about our personal lives and certain death.

*PRAYER: Great Author of life and Conqueror of death, we express our praise to You that both are under Your control, and that our times are in Your hands. Help us to draw on Your grace that we will be able to so live our lives that when death shall come we will be able to look back with peace and*

*confidence and ahead with faith and triumph! This we ask in
Jesus' name. Amen.*

---

WEEK 3:   Thursday
READ:   *Philippians 1:20-26 (look at verse 20)*

## PAUL'S ATTITUDE TOWARD LIFE OR DEATH

Now formulate the picture again—Paul is in prison, not
certain whether he will be permitted to live or be put to death.
He awakens to each morning (we know he was imprisoned at
least two years) with no lease on life. Caesar's stooges may allow
him to live one more day, or they may determine that he should
die. As the apostle expresses his ATTITUDE TOWARD LIFE
OR DEATH, it is comforting—maybe somewhat reassuring—
to hear him verbalize his ardent hope tinged with a slight touch
of apprehension. Read verse 20: "I eagerly expect and hope that
I will in no way be ashamed, but will have sufficient courage so
that now as always Christ will be exalted in my body, whether
by life or by death." Have you fabricated in your mind a Paul
who was almost inhuman? Have you thought that he never
sensed fear? That he never felt the very earthly feelings that
we experience periodically? It is apparent that he did. He was
deeply concerned that, whether he lived or whether he had to
face death, he would express no attitude or action that would
make him ashamed.

What was Paul's greatest passion through all of this uncertainty? That God release him from prison? No. His greatest desire was that, whether it be by living or whether it be by dying, "Christ (would) be exalted in (his) body." And in only one way could Christ be exalted in his body—Paul must "have sufficient courage"! But let us never forget that courage does not descend upon any of us automatically! And it did not chance upon Paul that way. If it had, it would not have been courage!

What is the concept expressed by the great apostle when he makes use of the word translated "courage"? The original thought is that of "openness, frankness, confidence, boldness." It certainly is not to say that Paul faced the issues of life and the stark reality of death without any twinge of anxiety at all. Recognizing his overwhelming drive to live and to preach the gospel, we may rest assured that Paul sensed some foreboding at the possibility of his impending death. It is to say, however, that right in that prison, in the very presence of such apprehension, he was able to exercise enough of the grace of God to be open and frank, confident and bold, in his forthright witness for Christ! That is true courage!

Is not this one of the besetting sins of the majority of present-day Christians? We allow our fears and timidity to paralyze us into cowardly silence instead of marshalling enough courage to overcome such feelings and be open and confident in sharing Christ.

We see one of the most magnificent incidents of courage in the Old Testament in the record of Nathan the prophet. Having become aware that David had committed adultery with Bathsheba and had contrived the murder of Uriah in order to cover his sin, he walked into the presence of that guilty king. Knowing full well that David had the power to take his life, but also knowing that he was under orders from his God, he presented to his ruler an illustration of one who had been blatantly unfair with his neighbor. David in anger declared, "As surely as the Lord lives, the man who did this deserves to die!" And Nathan, looking his king directly in the eye, responded, "You are the man!" (2

Samuel 12:1-14). Are we to assume that this prophet of God gave David that message without any human fear at all? I think not! David could have ordered him killed on the spot—and Nathan knew that! But he did what duty demanded in the very face of fear. This is Biblical courage!

So let us wrap up what Paul expresses in our text. His basic attitude toward life or death was this—whether it be through his living or through his dying, he deeply desired Christ to be exalted in his body. And that desire motivated his hope to live—and his willingness to die. He fully realized that in either case much courage would be required for him to continue to speak the message of Christ in his uncertain prison surroundings. And he did not want shame to be forced upon him by failing to articulate such witness. Thus he was fully expecting and hoping to continue to have such courage. Let us, too, endeavor always to exercise such a purpose to be faithful witnesses of our Lord and Savior, Jesus Christ! So be it forever!

*PRAYER: Dear heavenly Father, we are conscious that courage does not come automatically in the face of adverse circumstances. We thank You that the God who gave Paul grace to be faithful in his situation can do the same for us. We ask You to help us to exercise such boldness today to be Your true witnesses, and we will praise You for all of the positive results. Amen.*

*WEEK 3: Friday*
*READ: Philippians 1:20-26 again (note verse 21)*

## PAUL'S ASSESSMENT OF LIFE AND DEATH

Yesterday we discussed PAUL'S ATTITUDE TOWARD LIFE AND DEATH. Today we will focus our attention on PAUL'S ASSESSMENT OF LIFE AND DEATH. It is quite apparent that long before Paul experienced imprisonment he had fully appraised what both life and death had come to mean to him. And he bundles up these feelings into two sweeping expressions of faith.

First is his assessment of life—his statement speaks to the very heart and soul of the greatest dilemma many people encounter. They have never learned the true significance of being *alive* and *living!* Ben Robertson, in his book *Red Hills and Cotton*, tells of a tombstone near his boyhood home on which are inscribed the following words: "Born 1810. Died 1890. Lived 50 years."[1] George Bernard Shaw, notwithstanding all of the lasting good he accomplished in his life, as an old man and convinced that life was a "disease," concluded that the epitaph most appropriate for many men might read, "Died at thirty. Buried at sixty."[2] Channing Pollock has told of a man who confessed to him, "I'm a very lucky man! I am making a thousand dollars a day! So what? I haven't a friend in the world. It's a living death!"[3]

With much time on his hands in his Roman prison to evaluate and re-evaluate his convictions, Paul had boiled down life to what he considered to be its very basic ingredient: "For to me, to live is *Christ!*" That's it! Christ Jesus, to Paul, was the very fiber and core of *everything* that life offered! To him, Christ *was* life!

What, then, of his assessment of death? He says, ". . . and to

---

[1] From *Red Hills and Cotton* by Ben Robertson. Copyright © 1960 by University of South Carolina Press. Used by permission.

[2] From *A Treasury of Sermon Illustrations* edited by Charles L. Wallis. Copyright renewal © 1978 by Charles L. Wallis, p. 188. Used by permission of the publishers, Abingdon Press.

[3] *Ibid.*, p. 130

*JOY IN A ROMAN JAIL*        47

die *is gain!*" So, to the Christian, living or dying constitutes him a winner! To live is to have "Christ in us." To die is "to be present with the Lord." John Wesley used to say to those who questioned the brand of religion he preached, "Our people die well." His own mother became a prime example of her son's statement. Wesley wrote in his journal concerning her death, "We stood around the bed and fulfilled her last request: 'Children,' she said to them, 'as soon as I am released, sing a psalm of praise to God.'"[1]

D.L. Moody spoke exultantly to a group of friends: "Some morning you will read in the papers that D.L. Moody is dead. Don't believe a word of it! At that moment I shall be more alive than I am now. I was born of the flesh in 1837—I was born of the Spirit in 1856. That which is born of the flesh may die; that which is born of the Spirit shall live forever!"[2]

I do not suggest, nor does Paul, that we should live our lives hankering to die. Under normal circumstances, even the Christian tends to recoil from the article of death. Paul himself, in his first Corinthian epistle, branded death our "last enemy" (I Corinthians 15:26). But in today's text he intimates that, through the provision of Christ Jesus, our "last enemy, death," will be forced, ironically, to serve us in a friendly way—our very enemy will be compelled to usher us into the presence of our Savior! And that will be eternal gain!

Christian friend, let not life short-change you—"to live is *Christ!*" Let not death strike you with fear or doubt—"to die is *gain!*" By faith in the Lord Jesus, live out the fullness of your victory!

*PRAYER: Dear Father, thank you for the potential of living a full and useful life through Your Son, Jesus Christ. Help us to spend this day in a positive and victorious way so that*

[1] From *The Journal of John Wesley* edited by Percy Livingstone Parker, published by Moody Press, p. 100.

[2] From *The Life of Dwight L. Moody* by William R. Moody. Published by Fleming H. Revell Company, 1900, p. 554.

*someone, with whom we may converse, who has never found the secret of living, may come to understand the true answer to such a life—in Jesus' name. Amen.*

————————◆————————

WEEK 3:  *Saturday*
READ:  *Philippians 1:20-26 one more time (look at verses 20-26)*

## PAUL'S ALTERNATIVE BETWEEN LIFE AND DEATH

In verses 22-26 we are able to see PAUL'S ALTERNATIVE BETWEEN LIFE AND DEATH. We catch something of the tension he experienced, brought on by the tug between *duty* and *desire*. He had come to grips with both life and death in such a thorough and committed way that it had become very difficult for him to choose which he preferred.

I think it is important for us, however, as we read this section, to keep the author's circumstances clearly before us. Had Paul been free at the time of this writing to move, to preach openly and do the work of Christ in an unhindered way, I believe there would have been no question but that he would have certainly preferred to keep on living. But he was *not* free. He was in prison. In *this* state he discloses, "I am torn between the two." Why so? "I desire to depart and be with Christ, which is better by far." Nothing, absolutely nothing, could compare to "being with Christ." On the other hand, to continue living in the body would mean "more fruitful labor" for him. He was convinced that it was necessary for him to remain alive for the sake of the fellow believers in Philippi, that he might continue to help them progress joyfully in the Lord.

Though torn between the two, and while fully recognizing that the final choice as to whether he lived or died rested in the hands of God, nevertheless, an expectation on his part that he will keep on living *does* emerge in the text. He must be ready to die at a moment's notice, but Paul was making plans to *live!* Read it again. Convinced that it is "more necessary" for him to "remain in the body" for their sakes, he says, "I know that I will remain, and I will continue with all of you for your progress and joy in the faith, so that through my being with you again your joy in Christ Jesus will overflow on account of me." What a tremendous attitude!

We do not know whether Paul was ever permitted to return to Philippi again or not. It is not recorded that he did. But we do know that he was released from prison, and was allowed to preach openly again for a brief time before he was finally re-imprisoned and martyred for the cause of Christ. But through it all, Paul's attitude was one of *submission with expectation.* He was ready and willing to die. But he was planning to keep on living!

For the past three days we have examined PAUL'S ATTITUDE TOWARD LIFE OR DEATH, HIS ASSESSMENT OF LIFE AND DEATH and HIS ALTERNATIVE BETWEEN LIFE AND DEATH. It has not been difficult to ascertain the radical difference between his actual philosophy and his supposed philosophy ascribed to him by those who would accuse him, and all Christians, of being enamored with "pie in the sky—by and by—when we die." As Christians, let us keep our perspective clear —let us be completely ready to either live or die. But let us *plan* to live! And in expecting to live, let us purpose to expend the one life we have to the greatest glory possible to the name of our Savior, Jesus Christ.

*PRAYER: Living God, grant that today will be a day in which we will be able to "truly live." Help us to live with a zeal for*

*Christ. Grant us grace to invest this twenty-four hours help-*
*ing someone progress in their joy and faith. While we live this*
*day, and expect to live many more, never let us forget that this*
*one could be our last on earth, in Jesus' name. Amen.*

---

## THE CHRISTIAN AND THE GOSPEL
## OF CHRIST (1:27-30)

**Our Conduct Which Represents the Gospel (1:27)**
**Our Contention on Behalf of the Gospel (1:27B)**
**Our Courage in the Gospel (1:28)**
**Our Conflict Because of the Gospel (1:29-30)**

*WEEK 4: Sunday*
*READ: Philippians 1:27-30*

## THE CHRISTIAN AND THE GOSPEL OF CHRIST

To this juncture in his Philippian letter Paul has been very
personal in his remarks. He has exposed some of his deepest
inner feelings concerning his Christian friends. He has spoken
frankly of his imprisonment. He has dared to unfold his secret
hopes and anxieties involving living and dying.

At the point of today's text he begins to direct his remarks more specifically to the recipients of the epistle. His deep desire that the readers (both the Philippians and we who read today) imbibe positive attitudes and responses toward what he is about to say is self evident. With the exception of a brief section in chapter 2, verses 19-30 (where he speaks of Timothy and Epaphroditus), he will be directly challenging, rebuking, exhorting and praising those of us who read.

Most of his injunctions will be of a very practical nature, geared to challenging us to assume affirmative attitudes of obedience to God. He instructs us to guard against false doctrine, to strive for maturity and to be reconciled to each other, etc. On the other hand, in these down-to-earth "every day living" oriented remarks, much that is of a deeply doctrinal and theological nature also surfaces. But in order to maintain a proper perspective, let us continue to remind ourselves that, while the doctrinal concepts are clearly visible, his primary purpose is more pragmatic.

In verses 27-30, Paul commences the first of a number of such sections. He zeros in basically on what ought to be the Christian's response to God and life because of his peculiar relationship to the gospel of Christ. For the next four days we will involve ourselves with the following thoughts:

1. Concerning our conduct which represents the Gospel—Paul calls for CONSISTENCY.
2. Concerning our contention on behalf of the Gospel—Paul calls for UNITY.
3. Concerning our courage in the Gospel—Paul calls for BRAVERY.
4. Concerning our conflict because of the Gospel—Paul calls for DUTY.

Paul's motive in writing as he does is simple. He deeply yearns that the members of this church at Philippi, which he had founded, would continue to "go on" and grow spiritually in Christ Jesus. And he would speak the same to us! So let us study carefully and prayerfully that we may grow thereby and be more effective in our dedicated service to Christ.

*PRAYER: Father of our Lord Jesus Christ, we thank You for the gospel concerning Your Son. As we study about our relationship to this good news and what ought to be our attitudes and responses toward this message, we ask that You will guide us and empower us with Your Spirit. May such empowering result in true consistency and unity on our part, and in true bravery and the fulfilling of our duties to God. We ask this of You with thanksgiving. Amen.*

*WEEK 4: Monday*
*READ: Philippians 1:27-30 (focus on verse 27)*

## OUR CONDUCT WHICH REPRESENTS THE GOSPEL

In verse 27 Paul writes concerning the CHRISTIAN'S CONDUCT WHICH REPRESENTS THE GOSPEL—and he calls for CONSISTENCY. He says, "Whatever happens, conduct yourselves in a manner worthy of the gospel of Christ . . ." In the King James Version the word "conversation" is employed. Our present usage of that word has to do primarily with "the speaking of words." But in the 1600's, when the King James Version was translated the English word "conversation" referred more to "one's whole manner of behavior and conduct." The thought is made much clearer in other translations, including the New International Version which we are utilizing in this study. "Conduct yourselves (in your everyday life and behavior) in a manner worthy of the gospel of Christ," is Paul's injunction.

William Barclay, in his work on Philippians, calls special attention to the fact that the word translated "conduct yourselves" has the same meaning as to "be a citizen." The words rendered "city," "citizenship," "the place of one's citizenship" and this word all share the same root.[1] We have already noted that Philippi was founded as a Roman colony—citizens of Philippi were citizens of Rome. Philippi and all other Roman colonies were "little sections of Rome" scattered throughout the then known world. The inhabitants dressed as Romans, spoke the Latin language and called their rulers by Latin names. They were expected to conduct themselves as true citizens of Rome. They were in no way to bring shame upon their capital. Had Paul written to these Roman citizens saying, "Conduct yourselves as citizens of Rome," he would have utilized this word. His meaning, of course, would have been, "Be true representatives of the place of your citizenship."

These Philippian believers understood well the drive of Paul's statement—hopefully we can! In chapter 3 and verse 20, he reminds them and us that our citizenship (again the KJV has it "conversation") is in heaven! Though we now reside in a land "foreign" to that of our future abode, we are to conduct ourselves as loyal citizens of the place of our true citizenship. We are never to bring any disgrace upon that heavenly city. All that some people will ever know about heaven, and about God and His Son Jesus, is what you and I will represent to them through our everyday lives! May God help us!

Then catch the rather practical statement Paul makes: "Then, whether I come and see you, or only hear about you in my absence, I will know that you stand firm . . ." It is amazing what

---

[1]From _The Letters to the Philippians, Colossians, and Thessalonians_ (Revised Edition), translated and interpreted by William Barclay. Copyright © 1975 William Barclay. Published in the U.S.A. by The Westminster Press, p. 30. Used and adapted by permission.

motivates some people to "come across" as "sincere Christians." The whole atmosphere of many Christian homes changes radically when the members know the minister is coming. A certain pastor stopped to visit one of the families of his church. Mother, with her best foot forward, had served tea. Then it happened! Unexpectedly, her two junior aged sons came bursting through the back door. Before she could properly warn them that the "nice man who gives the sermons at the church" was there, the one began to holler, "Mom! Mom! You know that mangy old stray cat that you said you wished was dead? We caught him on the way home from school! I got him by the tail—and when he scratched me, I hit him and threw him down, and then Joey grabbed a big club and—" About that time he caught sight of the minister—and striking the most angelic pose that a junior aged boy could muster on short notice, he droned, "and then the dear Lord took him home to heaven." He had learned well "how to behave" when the preacher was present.

Paul is urging the Philippian believers to stand firm and to live truly genuine lives whether he is able to be among them or not. Their motivation to godliness must not be *his* presence, but *God's* presence! Likewise, concerning our conduct which represents the gospel, Paul is calling for consistency. "Conduct yourselves worthy of the gospel of Christ."

*PRAYER: Lord, we know that it is not our talk, but our walk that will bear true witness of the genuineness of our faith. Breathe Your Holy Spirit into our hearts anew today that we may have inner power to exemplify a proper type of conduct which will truly glorify You. We ask it in Jesus' name. Amen.*

WEEK 4: *Tuesday*
READ: *Philippians 1:27-30 again (give attention to verse 27b)*

## OUR CONTENTION ON BEHALF OF THE GOSPEL

Yesterday we discussed the first part of verse 27. Concerning OUR CONDUCT WHICH REPRESENTS THE GOSPEL, Paul calls for CONSISTENCY. Today look at the last part of the same verse where Paul speaks of OUR CONTENTION ON BEHALF OF THE GOSPEL, and calls for UNITY. He writes, "Then, whether I come and see you or only hear about you in my absence, I will know that you stand firm *in one spirit, contending as one man for the faith of the gospel.*"

Two issues concern Paul at this point: that these Philippian believers, and all of us who are true Christians, stand firm in our contention for the faith of the gospel; and that in our firmness in contending for the faith, we demonstrate one spirit as one man! We have, then, a double command. He calls for an uncompromising spirit! And he calls for a spirit of unity! And it is not always easy—yea, sometimes it can be very difficult—to mold both of these attributes into one human earth bound person! It becomes even more problematic to undertake the challenge of demonstrating sincerely both of these qualities in our behavior at the same time! And yet, that is what Paul is asking here.

Take that first characteristic—"Standing fast, contending for the faith of the gospel . . ." We are very much aware that our religious society does not lack for those who name the name of Christ and speak exaltingly of the Bible, who, nevertheless, deny both by their teachings and their lives. They deny the deity of Christ. They reject His virgin birth and the expiatory nature of His death on the cross. They disallow His literal resurrection from the dead and His second coming. They do not believe that we of necessity must be born again of the Spirit of God, and certainly not filled with the Holy Spirit. They do not accept the reality of sin or the certainty of a coming judgment.

They question the complete trustworthiness of the Bible.

Now to "contend for the faith" requires that there be *no compromise at all* concerning any of these truths. We are obligated to defend the clear teachings of the Scriptures at all cost.

But unnecessary problems bubble to the surface when we allow ourselves to become confused as to just what it is we are to defend and with whom we are to contend. We are to contend *for* "the faith of the gospel" *with* "those who oppose." We become sidetracked when we begin to contend for our own personal constricted ideas in the place of the gospel! We find ourselves devastating our own purposes when we begin to oppose *each other* rather than to unite with each other to contend with "those who oppose the gospel." Through the years one of the most frustrating facts with which we have been forced to grapple as sincere believers is this—we have become our own worst enemies much of the time! We have argued with each other over silly little nothings while the gospel suffered.

One fact Paul clarifies—if our witness is to be effective at all, there must first exist a spirit of unity among those who contend so uncompromisingly for the gospel! What, then, is unity? Is it the total lack of disagreement among God's people? Is unity uniformity? Does it smack of sameness? Not at all!

Paul describes such unity as being "in one spirit." This could very well mean, from the original, "in the one Holy Spirit." It most certainly involves "an agreement in spirit concerning the gospel of Jesus Christ" for which we contend!

And this can be realized notwithstanding areas of minor differences between us concerning various distinctives. Thus it is! Paul says we are to "stand firm"—"in one spirit"—"contending as one man"—"for the faith of the gospel"! Concerning our contention for the gospel, he pleads for unity. Let us take to heart his injunction.

*PRAYER: Dear Lord Jesus, sometimes it is so difficult to know how to "contend for the faith of the gospel" in an uncompromising way and "maintain a spirit of oneness" at the same time.*

*Grant us true wisdom and understanding so that we may be able to do both as unto the Lord, in whose name we pray. Amen.*

———————————◆‑◆‑◆———————————

WEEK 4:  *Wednesday*
READ:  *Philippians 1:27-30 again (take note of verse 28)*

## OUR COURAGE IN THE GOSPEL

Concerning a CHRISTIAN'S COURAGE IN THE GOSPEL, Paul calls for BRAVERY. In verses 27 and 28a we read these words: ". . . I will know that you stand firm in one spirit, contending as one man for the faith of the gospel *without being frightened in any way by those who oppose you.*" Does this statement contradict what Paul states in his first Corinthian letter that he himself experienced? In chapter 2 and verse 3 he confesses, "I came to you in weakness and *fear*, and with *much trembling.*" Again, in this very letter (Philippians), in verse 12 of chapter 2, he strongly urges, ". . . continue to work out your own salvation with *fear* and *trembling* . . ." Is this a refutation of his exhortation in our text? I think not!

A fragment of wisdom consists of being afraid at the proper time! Apparently Paul, too, recognized that there exists a time to have fear—as well as a time to exhibit no fear! At Philippi the enemies of the gospel of Christ were employing every method of intimidation they could marshal together in order to threaten the believers into silence and inactivity. Paul is as much as saying,

"Christians, ban together in a spirit of unity and stand firm in contending for the gospel! This is one time *not* to be afraid!"

What is it about those you know, who would oppose the gospel, that tends to badger you into silence, slamming the quietus on your testimony for Christ? Is it their financial status? their educational degree? their jeers? their threats? their friendship? Paul is calling upon you also to ". . . stand firm in one spirit, contending as one man for the faith of the gospel *without being frightened in any way* by those who oppose you!" Away with fear! Away with intimidation! Let God-given courage reign! Stand up in the power of the Spirit!

He goes on to state, "This (i.e. your courage) is a sign to them that they will be destroyed, but that you will be saved—and that by God." Your courage to stand firm in the midst of rebuff and to contend for the faith of the gospel when opposed is a proof of God's presence and favor with you and is a token of final victory! Let this fact be an encouragement to all of us! Concerning courage, Paul calls for bravery!

*PRAYER: Lord of battles, You have breathed into us Your Holy Spirit to give us spiritual power. Fill us anew with His presence, and help us to live in His power. Our paths will cross often with the paths of those who oppose the gospel. Help us not to be fearful, but to positively speak for the gospel and faithfully witness to its faith. Answer our prayer for Jesus' sake. Amen.*

## OUR CONFLICT BECAUSE OF THE GOSPEL

On Monday we read what Paul has written concerning OUR CONDUCT WHICH REPRESENTS THE GOSPEL where he called for CONSISTENCY. Tuesday we considered OUR CONTENTION ON BEHALF OF THE GOSPEL—Paul plead for UNITY. Yesterday we studied his statements involving OUR COURAGE IN THE GOSPEL as he urged us to BRAVERY.

Now today he speaks of OUR CONFLICT BECAUSE OF THE GOSPEL, and he lays upon us DUTY. He declares in verses 29 and 30, "For it has been granted to you on behalf of Christ not only to believe on Him, but also to suffer for Him, since you are going through the same struggle you saw I had, and now hear that I still have."

First, we need to appreciate the fact that Paul is not taunting us into a life of suffering for its own sake. Nor is he "courting" the idea of suffering. No special honor system exists for the one who adorns his testimony with a type of "spiritual badge" which displays the unmistakable message, "I am a Christian, and I want to suffer for Christ." Most of us know, to our chagrin, that a good share of the "sufferings" we have experienced has not been "for Christ's sake." Most have been brought on by our own lack of "good common sense"—as in the case of the inquirer who asked another quite sincerely, "Sir, are you one of those who call themselves 'Christians?'" To which the first replied, "Yes, I am—and if you are not, you'll go to hell fire as surely as you've asked me the question!" He could not understand then why his former associate shunned him. And he asked fellow Christians to pray for him, for he was being persecuted for Christ's sake.

On the other hand, let us also reckon with the fact that when a person becomes a bona fide Christian, his basic "groundwork for his convictions" begins to run completely diametrical to that of a society without Christ. His total lifestyle will, in fact, become contrary to that of the world system. And it is inevitable that what he believes and practices will sometime drive someone to react negatively—possibly even repugnantly—toward him. This may be very disturbing—even embarrassing—to some Christians. Especially new Christians can become extremely distraught, for instance, when friends let them know that if they are going to be so "narrow" as to refuse to participate in "our kind of partying," they need never come back to their home again!

"What shall we do in these cases?" they ask. I will tell you what they should do. They should do their *duty to God* first and foremost and humbly! That is what Paul is asking us to recognize in these verses. "It has been granted to (us) on behalf of Christ not only to believe on Him, but also to suffer for Him . . ."

In our comfortable America, we are not conditioned to the idea of suffering for much of *anything.* It has been cozy for us to develop the concept that becoming a Christian is the first step to a life of placidity. We follow through then by attending a respectable church with padded pews and air conditioning, listen to soothing songs and delightful sermons. And we form new friendships among people who like us!

Paul reminds us in our text that if we believe on Christ, it may mean that sometime we may also have to suffer for Him— and our Christian *duty* is to be willing to accept that fact and live for Christ *whatever* it may mean!

*PRAYER: Heavenly Father, we know so little of suffering for Your sake in this country. Help us not to be soft and flabby, spiritually. Grant us grace to be willing to "pay any price" You may require in order to live for You in an effective way, in Jesus' name. Amen.*

```
┌─────────────────────────────────────────────────┐
│                                                   │
│     THE MESSAGE OF CHRISTIAN UNITY (2:1-4)        │
│                                                   │
│     The Motives Toward Christian Unity (2:1)      │
│      The Meaning of Christian Unity (2:1-2)       │
│       The Marks of Christian Unity (2:3-4)        │
│                                                   │
└─────────────────────────────────────────────────┘
```

WEEK 4: Friday
READ: Philippians 2:1-4

## THE MESSAGE OF CHRISTIAN UNITY

We are now ready for chapter two in our study. In order to establish a proper frame of mind, recall that, in chapter one, Paul presses for the development of two characteristics on the part of Christians. The first has to do with developing a pattern of behavior that is worthy of the gospel of Christ. The second involves the necessity of Christian unity among God's people in contending for the faith of the gospel.

In chapter two then he develops both of these thoughts more completely. The first four verses form a simple, straightforward plea for a spirit of oneness. Verses 5 thru 11 demonstrate how Jesus Christ himself displayed such an attitude in His coming to earth—and Paul ties together both concepts of unity and obedient behavior in that section, enlarging on each. He then concentrates on the thought of obedience and behavior that is worthy of the gospel in verses 9 thru 18 where he helps us to understand how that behavior will aid us in relating to this present ungodly society.

First then, over the next three days, let us focus on this theme of unity as Paul treats it in verses 1 thru 4. It is apparent that some of the believers at Philippi could have been distant relatives of a few of the good standing members of any of our fundamental evangelical Bible believing churches today. It is quite obvious that a number had developed strong personal sentiments relating to certain aspects of religion. Sadly, they were far more intent on "proving the superior holiness of their own pet notions" than they were in "striving to create a true spirit of unity" among the body of believers.

And so, in these few verses, the writer issues a strong plea for these Christians—and for us—to develop and maintain this true attitude of Christian harmony among the members of the body. That is not to insinuate that Paul is insisting on agreement at the price of compromise with moral or ethical ideals! Oh no! But he is *un*compromising in his insistence that God's people ought to be striving for that spirit of *oneness in Christ* that is so necessary to the victorious on-going of the work of the Lord. And he would insist on this though it might call for a relaxing of one's hard headedness about non-essential personal perceptions!

I see three main concepts in these verses. On Saturday we will look at THE MOTIVES TOWARD CHRISTIAN UNITY. Sunday we will examine THE MEANING OF CHRISTIAN UNITY. On Monday our consideration will focus on THE MARKS OF CHRISTIAN UNITY. Let us prepare our hearts to allow God's Spirit to teach us how to do our part in helping to create an atmosphere that will foster such spiritual accord among the people with whom we identify.

*PRAYER: Dear Lord Jesus, before Your crucifixion, You prayed for all of Your own that we might be one, even as You and Your Father are one. We want to see that prayer truly answered in our lives. As we study this section of Your Word, please help us to know better how to have and maintain a true spirit of unity among Your people. We ask this for Your dear sake. Amen.*

## THE MOTIVES TOWARD CHRISTIAN UNITY

In verse 1 of today's reading, Paul *assumes* that if one has been united with Christ certain benefits will result. And he further assumes that these very benefits ought then to motivate that believer to strive for Christian unity. The purpose of his use of the word "if" in verse 1 is not to create doubt, but rather to establish the credibility of the stated fact. It has the effect of saying, *"Since* certain facts are true, various results ought then to follow."

Let me illustrate. I may ask of you, "Are you happy?" To which you might reply, "Yes, I am very happy!" And my response could suggest, "If you are happy, let your face show it." I do not mean by that injunction to question your bliss. The drive of the statement is rather, *"Since* you are happy, such joy ought to prompt you to allow your face to exhibit that fact."

Such is the purpose of Paul's statement in today's text! He is asserting, "You are united to Christ by faith and certain benefits have resulted. *Since* these blessings are yours, let them motivate you to make my joy complete by your striving for Christian unity among yourselves."

Now, what are these benefits? *Encouragement* is one. *Comfort* is another. A third is *fellowship* and *tenderness* a fourth. *Compassion* is yet a fifth. Let us attempt to comprehend his entire thought by reading verses 1 and 2 together: "If you have any encouragement from being united with Christ, if any comfort from His love, if any fellowship with the Spirit, if any tenderness and compassion, then make my joy complete by being like-minded, having the same love, being one in spirit and purpose."

So we confront the challenge that while being "united with Christ" is, in fact, designed to graciously benefit our own hearts and lives, these favors are not an end in themselves. To be "encouraged" and "comforted" certainly ought to mean much to us. To experience the "fellowship of the Spirit" is precious to one's heart. "Tenderness" of soul and a "compassionate spirit" are attitudes which every Christian ought to deeply covet. But these blessings ought not be entirely subjective. We must guard continually that we do not become totally self-centered in our very enjoyment of these advantages of salvation! Egocentric Christians (whose *only* driving concerns are "that *I* may be encouraged" and "that *I* may enjoy the comfort of His love" or even that *I* may be the primary recipient in "my fellowshipping in the Spirit") can become very selfish—even repulsive—in their Christian outlook and practice. Lord, save us from that type of short-sighted Christianity!

These Christian benefits, while to be greatly enjoyed and appreciated, ought also serve as MOTIVES TOWARD CHRISTIAN UNITY. Paul's concern is that these privileges prompt us to view very realistically our relationships with *each other*. And as we do so, we ought to be careful to strive continually for that *true* spiritual oneness which binds God's people together in purpose and love.

*PRAYER: Dear Lord, we thank You for these wonderful joys of salvation which we have studied today, and for all of the other blessings we enjoy through Christ. Out of appreciation for such, help us to "be at one" with our brothers and sisters in Christ today. Amen.*

## THE MEANING OF CHRISTIAN UNITY

Yesterday we noted THE MOTIVES TOWARD CHRISTIAN UNITY. Today we shall consider THE MEANING OF CHRISTIAN UNITY. Paul has enumerated five *motives* for such unity in verse 1 as he builds toward identifying its meaning in verse 2. This meaning is brought into focus by a threefold description: "be like-minded," "have the same love," "be one in spirit and purpose." So one has to do with our *mind*, another with our *love* and yet a third with our *spirit*.

Now, first, what does Paul envision when he says, "be like-minded"? Does he intend to insinuate that for Christians to possess true unity it is necessary that we all "think alike" about every detail of the various issues we face in life? If so, whose thinking among us shall become the measuring rod? mine? yours? someone else's? What brand of unity would result if such concord must depend upon all others coming to agree with our peculiar opinions? Or our coming to concede to others? That is not at all Paul's intent here!

The word Paul employs denotes more a "way or method of thinking." It signifies a "set or frame of mind." The New International Version has focused on the idea clearly in the last phrase: "one in purpose." It most certainly is quite feasible for two persons to strongly disagree with each other, theologically or practically, and at the same time share very sincerely the same "set of mind" or "inner purpose." Both may deeply desire to glorify Jesus Christ, their Savior and Lord! This is precisely what Paul visualizes when he says, "be like-minded." And such is one very genuine characteristic of true Biblical unity!

What then is involved in "having the same love"? The particular love to which Paul refers here is that type which is breathed into our hearts by the Spirit of God. And one *proof* that such professed love is truly possessed in the heart is observed in the fact that it will prompt us to *exercise* such God-given devotion and affection toward our brothers and sisters in Christ. And this also can be realized, notwithstanding the fact that we probably will not always totally agree with each other concerning every detail of Christian doctrine and practice! Celcus, a critic of early Christians, said of them, "These Christians love each other even before they are acquainted!"[1] Ah true! But how much more significant when this love in our hearts helps us to be loyal to each other even *after* we are acquainted! That is unity!

How else does Paul describe this Christian unity? "Being one in spirit" or "united in spirit as one." He refers here primarily to "disposition." We ought to always be striving to manifest the same type of disposition—that is, I repeat again, a mind bent to glorify Jesus Christ!

So we see in our text what I call Paul's description of the *meaning* of Christian unity—one mind, one love, one spirit. Lord, may it ever be among Your people!

*PRAYER: Lord, even as You and the Father are one, so grant us, Your mortal children, the inner power to be one! Mold our minds, fire our love and quicken our spirits that together we may, in a very Biblical way, glorify Jesus Christ our Savior in whose name we pray. Amen.*

---

[1]From *A Treasury of Sermon Illustrations* edited by Charles L. Wallis. Copyright renewal © 1978 by Charles L. Wallis, p. 195. Used by permission of the publishers, Abingdon Press.

## THE MARKS OF CHRISTIAN UNITY

The past two days we have discussed THE MOTIVES TOWARD CHRISTIAN UNITY and THE MEANING OF CHRISTIAN UNITY. Today we are going to look at verses 3 and 4 where Paul clarifies some of THE MARKS OF CHRISTIAN UNITY involving our behavior toward each other.

A genuine spirit of Christian unity cannot allow for selfishness or pride. Such egocentric attitudes certainly tend to ruin happy relationships with others and are prone to divide instead of unify. In verse 3, he says, "Do nothing out of selfish ambition or vain conceit." These words could be rendered, "Do nothing by way of *rivalry* or *vainglory*." What is the most common method Satan utilizes to tear down a spirit of unity among God's people? Fragment the camp! He did it in Paul's day at Corinth. Some followed Cephas; others, Apollos. A third party lauded Paul while still another claimed to be "of Christ." These divisions resulted in envying, strife and rivalry. It happens among us also! An over reaction on the part of some to the different opinions held by others concerning some minor doctrinal stance, or a certain required behavior pattern, or some method of ministry is usually enough to set off the "dissecting process." Instead of simply purposing to *accept* one's fellow Christians and *believe* in their sincerity, the expected reaction is that each will "choose a side" and "take a stand." One segment assumes that its "religious duty" is to prove the others wrong and themselves right. It seems "obvious" to them that their opinion is more spiritual than that of the others and certainly more blessed of God! What results? Rivalry! Conceit in one's own "correctness"! Spiritual smugness! I believe that is precisely what Paul has in mind in our text!

I recall vividly an oversized discussion which broke out on the campus of Bethel College in Mishawaka, Indiana, while I was a student there. It concerned the college's proposed entrance into an inter-collegiate sports program. A number of students were strongly convinced, quite sincerely if mistakenly, that such a program on a Christian College campus would unquestionably detract from its positive testimony. Little camps formed, each feeling "more spiritually motivated" than the other. I will never forget the reaction of one student (who now, to the praise of God, is in full-time Christian education, well respected, and has long since changed his attitude). He was embroiled in heated debate with a group of students in one of the halls. As the discussion reached its crescendo, he raised his voice: "All right, we're going to settle this once and for all." Drawing an imaginary line across the corridor, he challenged his listeners in the most noble of tones, "Those who agree with me step across this line! We'll see who the really spiritual students are!" I confess with embarrassment that I, too, participated in that "face off"! We all failed to comprehend that God was far more deeply concerned with the *"rivalry"* and *"spiritual conceit,"* so pronounced among us, than He was with the proposed sports program. Christian unity will not allow for such selfishness or pride, for it is hell-bent on ruining relationships between God's people.

Again, Christian unity will force us to recognize the genuine worth of other Christians, notwithstanding such possible differences of opinions: "In humility, consider others *better* than yourselves." Would it shock you one day to discover that the person with whom you so vehemently disagree involving some doctrinal discussion or some issue concerning behavior, is, in fact, living closer to God than you? Would it shake your spiritual security to find that he is demonstrating more practical fruit of the Spirit than you do? Paul is asserting in our text that the only safe attitude to assume, in a spirit of Christian oneness, is to consider that others, at least in some point of Christian maturity, have surpassed us, and have something deeply spiritual to offer us! *Can we accept this?*

Finally, true Christian unity will prompt us to develop a

genuine interest in the concerns of others: "Each of you should look not only to your own interests, but also to the interests of others." Is it not humiliating to us as Bible believing Christians that we must confess that, by far, the vast majority of our time, effort, planning, work, interest, vitality and drive is thrown in the direction of concerns which are entirely self-centered? Must we not admit that we invest very little time and effort into just plain "showing interest" in the daily problems of others? Friends are admitted into the hospital, neighbors have babies, acquaintances die, new people attend our church, a couple moves into the community, families pass through crises, graduations come and go, honors are bestowed, and on and on—and we are so totally preoccupied with our own interests, that few of these circumstances faze us much at all! Paul says that one of the primary marks of true Christian unity is a genuine caring interest in others and their joys and hurts!

So here are three marks of Christian unity—lack of selfish ambition and conceit, recognition of the genuine worth of other believers and a sincere interest in the concerns of others. May we strive to develop these evidences of noble character which make for such unity!

*PRAYER: Lord, how much we need the indwelling presence of the Holy Spirit in order to develop such marks of character! Fill us anew with His fullness and power, and help us to ever be striving to be "one" with our fellow believers. We ask this in Jesus' name. Amen.*

WEEK 5:  Tuesday
READ:  Philippians 2:5-11

## THE ATTITUDE OF CHRIST

Our scripture lesson for today develops an extremely enlightening and challenging segment of the Word of God in which Paul exposes our thinking to the basic mind frame of Christ from three perspectives. We see, first, His attitude toward His original position in heaven. We then observe the mental posture He demonstrated in coming to this earth. Finally, His disposition toward His exaltation back to heaven is disclosed.

And this total description of the spirit of Christ is inserted into a section where Paul is issuing a strong plea to the Christians at Philippi (and to us) to strive for true Christian unity and loyal obedience to God. He is asserting that the mood which Christ maintained is that which we as Christians ought to evidence in order to make for oneness among Christians and to prompt obedience to God as an effective and integral part of our lives.

The core statement of the entire section is found in verse 5: "Your *attitude* should be the same as that of Christ Jesus." The King James translators have rendered this verse, "Let this *mind* be in you which was also in Christ Jesus." He is not, of course, demanding that we have the same intelligence which Christ had—that would be impossible! His idea is that of "disposition," "attitude," "spirit," "frame of thought." It could be translated, "May *the same spirit* which was in Christ Jesus be in you."

Then for the next six verses he enlarges on how the spirit of Jesus affected Him as He came to earth, and how that "thought framework" inspired the heavenly Father to respond. And so for the next three days, while we are considering this attitude of Christ and the resulting reaction on the part of the Father, let us constantly hear these opening words of verse 5: "May the same spirit which was in Christ Jesus be in you."

We will look then at the attitude of Christ from three standpoints. On Wednesday we will evaluate His attitude in HIS SUPREME POSITION in heaven. On Thursday our attention will be placed on his attitude in HIS SELFLESS CONDESCENSION to earth. And on Friday we will note His attitude in HIS SUBLIME EXALTATION back to heaven.

As we prayerfully study this section, let us request of the Holy Spirit His special insight in order to learn how to make the disposition of Christ our own mind set. Let us ask Him then to help us to know how to demonstrate that attitude in our everyday lives. Even so, Amen!

*PRAYER: Dear Father, we recognize that our attitudes are not always those of Jesus. Grant us forgiveness. Help us to learn how to develop a frame of mind toward the will of God that would be comparable to His. Bathe our minds in the Holy Spirit and help us this day to exemplify our Savior well. We ask this in Jesus' name. Amen.*

## HIS SUPREME POSITION

In today's reading, Paul lays a foundation designed to aid us in appreciating more fully the total attitude of Christ toward the will of God. He does this by first revealing His original disposition in eternity past toward HIS SUPREME POSITION in heaven. In verse 6 we read, "Who being in very nature God did not consider equality with God something to be grasped . . ." Actually the King James rendering is probably closer to the literal thought at this point: "Who, being in the form of God, thought it not robbery to be equal with God . . ."

Note carefully these loaded phrases: "In very nature God," or "in the form of God"—and again, "not robbery to be equal with God." We are looking at a strong statement affirming the divinity and Godhead of Jesus Christ. We observe a picture of Jesus in eternity past in His exalted position, identified with the very eternal God. He is declared to have been "in the very form of God," "equal with God" and "one with God"! And in such a position, He "thought it not robbery to be equal with God"! In the original, this last assertion may warrant one of two meanings, either one of which possesses the same drive—that of equality with God! It may mean that Christ did not have to "snatch at" equality with God, because He really possessed it as an inherent right. He did not have to "rob" God to hold such equality. Or it could mean that He did not clutch at such equality as if to "hug it jealously to His breast." Phillips has preferred that thought in his translation: "For he who had always been God by nature did not cling to his privileges as God's equal."[1]

In either case His equality with God in form and nature and position shines through clearly! He enjoyed the highest position

---

[1] J.B. Phillips, translator: *The New Testament in Modern English*, Revised Edition. Copyright © J.B. Phillips 1958, 1960, 1972. Used by permission of Macmillan Publishing Company.

that heaven could afford and recognize. John 1:1 substantiates this truth: "In the beginning was the Word, and the Word was with God, and the Word was God." Again, when Jesus entered this world, born of a virgin, the angel said, quoting the Old Testament: " 'They will call him Immanuel'—which means, 'God with us' " (Matthew 1:23).

As we consider the spirit of Christ tomorrow and on Friday, let us keep ever before us His pre-incarnate supreme position, for this original status will enhance everything Paul has to say about His willingness then to fully identify with man, to be fully clothed in human flesh and bone.

Let us continue to hear Paul say, "Let this attutide be in you, which was also in Christ Jesus." When Christ yielded to the heavenly Father and laid aside His heavenly glory and condescended to come to earth, He submitted to the will of God as one who was "equal with God." We are asked to surrender to God, not as those who are equal with God, but as human beings. If the One who was equal with God was so willing to sacrifice His exalted position to obey His Father, how much more should we be willing to "let this attitude be in us"? May God give us His help.

_PRAYER: Dear heavenly Father, as we recognize who Christ is and the attitude He was willing to formulate toward Your plan and purpose in the world, it breeds in us a desire to have that same frame of mind. Help us this day to truly yield to the will of God. Help us to live out that yielded attitude in our lives and may Jesus Christ this day be magnified through our submission to Thee. We ask this in Jesus' name. Amen._

WEEK 5: *Thursday*
READ: *Philippians 2:5-11 a second time (look especially at verses 7-8)*

## HIS SELFLESS CONDESCENSION

Now recall our study of yesterday, keeping in mind Christ's SUPREME POSITION in heaven from whence He humbled himself. With that tremendous truth as our backdrop then, today we will concentrate on HIS SELFLESS CONDESCEN- SION to earth. Note carefully verse 7: "But (he) made himself nothing, taking the very nature of a servant, being made in human likeness . . ." Again, the literal rendering is graphic: "He *emptied himself*, taking the form of a slave, becoming in the likeness of men . . ." The words in the NIV rendered "made himself nothing" embrace the vivid idea "to pour out until nothing is left, to completely empty."

But let us not misinterpret this statement! Of what did Jesus empty himself? His deity? His sinlessness? His perfection? Not at all! In fact, it was quite the opposite. While maintaining His deity, His sinlessness and His perfection, *He emptied himself of His heavenly position*—of the reputation and glory of that position. He emptied himself of the freedom of an eternal heavenly state. From the eons past, He had never known the confines of being bound in a human body of flesh and bone with the possibilities of pain, sorrow, loneliness or weariness. But, in obedience to the everlasting plan of God, He took on himself all of this willingly.

And being clothed in a human body, *He emptied himself of His impeccability.* He could now be tempted, and was! Yea, He "has been tempted in every way, just as we are—yet was without sin" (Hebrews 4:15). From forever past, He had never encountered the first trace of temptation. But He laid that privilege aside.

Beyond all this, *He emptied himself of His right of rulership.* He who formerly had maintained the right to be served by

JOY IN A ROMAN JAIL                                              75 legions of angels, emptied himself of that prerogative and "took upon himself the very nature of a servant."

Let's bundle it all up in the words of verse 7b: He was "made in human likeness." Through the mystery of the incarnation, which we will never be able to fully comprehend, the second person of the God-head became man! He clothed himself with a human body! He did not cease to be God! But He did truly become man! He took the long step down from the heavenly to the earthly, fully identifying with mankind, being born of the virgin Mary.

But when Jesus became a human being, His example of humility and condescension had only begun. As a man "He humbled himself." To what extent? To "obedience." What kind of obedience? He was "obedient to death." What type of death? "Even death on a cross!" When Christ consented to death, He embraced mortality. When He subscribed to the cross, He stooped to ignomy! Crucifixion in Paul's day constituted the most loathsome death possible, reserved for the lowest of criminals—an emblem of utter shame and reproach.

Now do not lose the underlying drive of this whole section. As we read Paul's statement concerning this unfolding attitude on the part of Christ in yieldedness to the Father, let us be reminded of his opening words of this segment: "Your attitude should be the same as that of Christ Jesus." Paul, in our text, is saying, "Christians at Philippi (and everywhere), remember that in all the wide universe, never in a million ages, has there been such a demonstration of self emptying! If Christ did that, we too ought to be willing to manifest the same disposition and yieldedness to God."

For Jesus, the climactic crisis in His yieldedness to the Father, was reached in the Garden of Gethsemane. There He prayed desperately, "If it is possible, may this cup be taken from me. Yet not as I will, but as you will" (Matthew 26:39). There is seen the crux of yieldedness to God!

To share "the same attitude He had," must certainly involve the same type of yieldedness on our part to the will of God.

We, His children, must carefully and conscientiously weigh "His will" beside "our will." And at every juncture where these two conflict, we must say "yes" to His will and "no" to our will. Say it often in the quietness and honesty of your inner soul: "I give myself entirely to God and His will. I yield my all to Him, gladly and sincerely! I renounce selfishness and self-centeredness! I declare Christ to be my all in all." This is the attitude of Christ. May it ever be our attitude as well! Amen!

*PRAYER: Dear Father, we see the attitude of Christ and we recognize our own basic attitude. To maintain the attitude of our Lord Jesus is not always easy—certainly not an automatic result of being a Christian. Help us this day to once again say one total "yes" to You. Assist us then to "live out" that attitude of submission to You and Your plan. We ask it in Jesus' name. Amen.*

———————————◆———————————

WEEK 5: *Friday*
READ: *Philippians 2:5-11 one final time (give attention to verses 9-11)*

### HIS SUBLIME EXALTATION

On Wednesday we noted the attitude of Christ in HIS SUPREME POSITION in heaven. On Thursday we thought on His attitude involving HIS SELFLESS CONDESCENSION to earth. Now today we will consider HIS SUBLIME EXALTATION BACK TO HEAVEN. In verse 9 we read, "Therefore God exalted Him to the highest place, and gave Him a name that is above every name, that at the name of Jesus every knee should bow." The honor and the glory which Christ has received, is receiving, and will yet receive in the future is two-fold as Paul states it in our text. First, there is the honor which *God* bestows. Second, there is the honor which *others* bestow.

Let us first, then, contemplate the honor and glory received from God himself. "God (has) exalted Him to the highest place, and gave Him a name that is above every name . . ." By His own mighty power, God the Father has openly stamped His seal of honor on His Son by exalting Him to the highest position heaven can afford. He stands in shining array in the heavenlies, declared to be the eternal Son of God! The resurrection is part of this glory! The ascension shares in making up part of this glory! His enthonement as the everlasting mediator further enhances the total picture! Thus, Jesus laid aside His heavenly position only to receive it again. He relinquished His rulership only to take it up again. In His sublime exaltation, His heavenly Father has given it all back again, now enlarged and intensified.

There is also, secondly, the glory and honor He receives from others. Christ is magnified every time a sinner turns from sin and gives his faith and fidelity to Him as Savior and Lord. He is further glorified when that new convert begins to evidence a transformed life. He is greatly honored when he yields his all in full consecration and is filled with the sanctifying Holy Spirit and begins to manifest the fruit of a Spirit-filled life. But this is only the beginning! Paul is referring in our text, more specifically, to a coming day when God will assemble all the redeemed of all ages in the heavenlies, and a celestial coronation will take place. These will fall before Him! And as the saved of all ages bow in honor of Christ, angels also will bend the knee—for "every knee . . . in heaven" will bow! The whole heavenly world will give Him the honor and the glory due unto His name!

But there is yet more! Today there still live men and women who refuse to yield in surrender to that name. But Paul is affirming here that on that day *every knee* will, in fact, bow in open submission and confession! That forced confession will come too late to save them, but they *will* bow and they *will* confess that Jesus is Lord! Not only will *they* confess, but the *demons* of hell will be forced to bow, for Paul says every knee will bow "in heaven and on earth and under the earth"—oh, yes,—even those "under the earth," (referring to fallen angels) will give Him honor!

*All* shall bow, and *"every tongue shall confess* that Jesus Christ is Lord to the glory of God." Have you followed his entire thought? Paul says, "Your attitude should be the same as that of Christ . . ."—a disposition to do the whole will of God. Then he describes the attitude of Christ. He was equal with God but He emptied himself and became a man. As a man, He humbled himself to obedience, even to the death of the cross! Therefore, God has exalted Him, and some day the whole creation will openly acknowledge His worthiness! The intimation is that if we share His same disposition while on earth, someday we, too, shall share in His exaltation in the heavenlies, "heirs of God and co-heirs with Christ" (Romans 8:17). Let this truth motivate us to a total submission to God and His will. And in such an attitude of full consecration, let us allow the purifying Holy Spirit to demonstrate His holiness in our lives.

*PRAYER: Oh, Thou exalted Christ, grant us the grace this day to understand fully that Your exaltation was preconditioned upon Your submission to Your heavenly Father. Grant us the grace to have this same attitude toward our own heavenly Father. Teach us submission and yieldedness to the total will of God in Jesus' name we pray. Amen.*

```
┌─────────────────────────────────────────────────┐
│                                                   │
│         A CALL TO OBEDIENCE (2:12-18)             │
│                                                   │
│          Cooperation with God (2:12)              │
│        Inspiration from God (2:12-13)             │
│          Obligation to God (2:14-15)              │
│        Illumination for God (2:15-18)             │
│                                                   │
└─────────────────────────────────────────────────┘
```

*WEEK 5: Saturday*
*READ: Philippians 2:12-18*

## A CALL TO OBEDIENCE

A little boy was asked, "How did it happen that you fell out of bed, Joey?" To which Joey replied, "I musta' fell out of bed because I fell asleep too close to where I got in." I believe the reason so many Christians "take a fall," spiritually, is because they "fall asleep" too close to where they get in.

In our text today, Paul is urging the Philippian Christians (and all Christians) to guard against such spiritual lethargy by simply continuing to obey Jesus Christ. Now let's review a little. In this total section (1:27 through 2:18), Paul is urging true believers to strive for two moral goals: Christian unity and Christian obedience. Concerning Christian unity he has said in chapter one, "Stand firm *in one spirit*," and "contend *as one man* for the faith of the gospel." And in chapter two he has developed the theme of such unity more completely. He has enlarged our concept of the very attitude of Christ and has pressed us to share that same disposition. Such a mind set will certainly tend toward true spiritual unity—unity in the Spirit and unity with others who participate in such yieldedness to the Father.

In today's text, then, he develops the thought of Christian obedience. Here is revealed the human responsibility we share as Christians to simply, but carefully, comply with God—and that continually, day by day! Christian, recognizing that we are saved by grace, let us never be so careless as to imagine the *grace* of God to be designed to exempt us from *obedience* to God. Grace was never intended to absolve us of our known duty to God. Let us confess to each other often that there is no adequate substitute for simple, careful, sincere, loving obedience to our heavenly Father.

Paul says in our text, "Therefore, my dear friends (literally, 'beloved ones'), as you have always *obeyed*—not only in my presence, but now much more in my absence—continue . . ." In the context of this section of Scripture, I see four thoughts develop concerning Christian obedience. We shall consider these thoughts in our study for the next four days. On Sunday we will evaluate our COOPERATION WITH GOD and on Monday, our INSPIRATION FROM GOD. On Tuesday, then, we will face our OBLIGATION TO GOD, and on Wednesday our ILLUMINATION FOR GOD will form our theme.

As we ponder this significant section of God's Word, let us be asking the Lord to teach us the utter importance of living a life of dedicated obedience to Him. And let us examine our own lives to be certain that we are truly exemplifying in our daily living what we say we believe is so important.

*PRAYER: Dear heavenly Father, we recognize the grace of God and appreciate its work in our hearts and lives. By Your grace, give us inner help this day to walk in obedience before our Savior. And help us to do so out of love. We ask it in Christ's name, for our good, and for Your glory. Amen.*

## COOPERATION WITH GOD

Paul's contention in today's reading is that, in a life of obedience, our COOPERATION WITH GOD is a vital necessity. He calls for such a practice of agreeing with God in verse 12: ". . . as you have always obeyed—not only in my presence, but now much more in my absence—continue to work out your salvation with fear and trembling . . ."

Do you have a problem with Paul's statement here? Does it appear to you that he tends to contradict here what he teaches concerning "salvation by faith" in Romans? There is no contradiction at all. The original word in our text which is translated "work out" involves the thought of "bringing to completion" or "working fully." The idea is that we Christians must "fully work" or "bring to completion" what we have come already to possess by way of salvation in our hearts. The concept is the same as expressed in Ephesians 2:8-10: "For it is by grace you have been saved, through faith—and this not from yourselves, it is the gift of God—not by works so that one can boast. For we are God's workmanship, created in Christ Jesus *to do good works*, which God prepared in advance for us to do." WE have been saved by faith through the grace of God alone! But having been saved by faith, we are to then express that faith in the performance of good works! We are to "work out in our lives" what He has worked in us by faith.

So the first issue we must face is this—before we can "work fully" or "bring to completion" our salvation, that salvation must, first of all, have been "worked in" us by the Holy Spirit of God. We might ask the same question a little girl asked her mother after listening to a very legalistic sermon on "salvation by works" from this very text. Her pastor insisted that we cannot be saved by grace alone, but must "work out our own salvation." Innocently the girl asked her mother, "Mommy, how can you work it out if you haven't got it in?"[1] And that is precisely the question!

We cannot afford to disregard the fact that when God relates to those who have been saved by grace He is not dealing with dangling puppets suspended on the end of a divine string. God is a moral God! And He interacts with moral people—free agents who possess the power of negative or positive choice—hence, the God-given responsibility to "work out our own salvation"! And how is that to be accomplished? Our context states that it is by "obedience." Obedience to what? To the "attitude of Christ" of which he has spoken in verses 5 through 11. And that obedience dare not be a careless, half-hearted brand. "Continue to work out your salvation *with fear and trembling.*" That is not a morbid, neurotic fear. Paul Rees has caught the pulse of that phrase. He tells of a surgeon who, after 25 years of practice, still felt the tension mount and reach its peak as he scrubbed up every time before a surgery—then subside into calmness as he took the instrument into his hand.[2] That type of fear is healthy. It does not paralyze its subject. It drives him to prudent action. I believe Phillips unveils something of the mental perspective of Paul here by translating those final words of verse 12 as follows: ". . . with a proper sense of awe and responsibility."[3]

So Paul speaks of the necessity of our cooperation with God—a type of cooperation which will manifest itself through a life of total obedience to the will of God as we honestly comprehend it.

*PRAYER: Dear Father in heaven, we know that obedience*

---

[1]From *Philippians* by H.A. Ironside. Copyright © 1978 by Loizeaux Brothers, p. 49. Used by permission.

[2]From *The Adequate Man* by Paul S. Rees. Copyright © 1959 by Fleming H. Revell Company, p. 51. Used by permission.

[3]J.B. Phillips, translator: *The New Testament in Modern English*, Revised Edition. Copyright © J.B. Phillips 1958, 1960, 1972. Used by permission of Macmillan Publishing Company.

*to You does not come automatically. Our cooperation is completely necessary. Grant us the grace this day, in love to Christ, to simply obey You with all of our hearts in everything, in Jesus' wonderful name. Amen.*

❧

———————————◆◆◆———————————

WEEK 6:  Monday
READ:  *Philippians 2:12-18 again (look at verses 12-13)*

## INSPIRATION FROM GOD

Yesterday we saw that COOPERATION WITH GOD is a necessity if we purpose to obey Him properly. Now today, in connection with the matter of obedience again, Paul encouragingly speaks of our INSPIRATION FROM GOD: "Continue to work out your salvation with fear and trembling, *for it is God who works in you to will and to do what pleases Him."*

Here is the secret of our abiding victory in Christ Jesus! Here is the divine mastery of a yielded will! As our will is kept submitted to the will of God, the fact is, God himself begins to operate in and through that yielded will. And as God works in us, He breathes into our hearts both the desire and the dynamic to do what He wants us to do! He gives both the motivation and the activation. When we surrender our power of volition completely and continually to the control of Jesus Christ, God, in response and by the Holy Spirit, transforms our very inner desires. He implants in us a "God-given want-to" to do the whole will of God! Read it again: "For it is God who works in you to will (that is the desire, the motivation and power to will) and do what pleases Him (that is the dynamic, the activation and power to work)."

But let us not misdirect Paul's words here. This is not predestined divine determinism! This is not God working in us in spite of our will—this is God operating in us in cooperation with our will. We do violence both to the character of God and the character of man (as well as to the very intent of this text) to assume that Paul is declaring that God forces man to desire what he does not want to desire or to do what he would refuse to do! That is not at all the thought. The simple truth is this—when we fulfill verse 12 by a constant, willing, yielded obedience to the attitude of Christ, we may fully trust Christ to fulfill verse 13 in us through the inworking power of His Spirit. That is true inspiration and we may fully expect such inspiration to come from God.

Let us, by faith, draw upon that divine motivation today! Let us allow God, by His Holy Spirit, to breathe into our hearts an ever-deepening, driving desire to do what pleases Him! So help us, Lord Almighty!

PRAYER: Thou dynamic God of heaven, grant us this day the inner motivation and power to do what pleases You. Thank you for Your Holy Spirit who so works in our hearts that such a marvelous change of drive and direction can be very practical and real to us. Let this be so today that our lives will demonstrate Christ, in Jesus' name. Amen.

*WEEK 6: Tuesday*
*READ: Philippians 2:12-18 once again (notice verses 14-15)*

## OBLIGATION TO GOD

Yesterday and the day before we considered two thoughts in our study involving obedience to God: OUR COOPERATION WITH GOD and OUR INSPIRATION FROM GOD. Now again today, in connection with this subject, Paul speaks of OUR OBLIGATION TO GOD. Read verse 14: "Do everything without complaining or arguing so that you may become blameless and pure, children of God without fault in a crooked and depraved generation." Here is the earthy, practical part of this whole section—the segment which has to do with the everyday grind of cranking out proper attitudes under circumstances which do not adequately set the stage for such reactions.

Now let us keep the total thought of this entire section in proper perspective. In verses 1-4 of this chapter we saw Paul's deep concern that Christian unity prevail among God's people. He followed then in verses 5-11 with a strong appeal to us to embrace the same attitude and disposition Jesus did. Our text today is part of a segment (verses 12-18) where we hear a clarion call to obedience—and today's verses once again stress practical unity. It sounds as though Paul is trying to help us to understand that a willingness to maintain the attitude of Jesus and a willingness to simply and sincerely obey God will help pave the way to the true Christian unity which he called for back in verses 1-4! But now he fingers an added dimension. He says that we should do it all "without complaining or arguing"—i.e. "without grumbling and controversies." So here is a call to obedience apart from griping! This is the nitty-gritty of the whole section, and quite likely involves much more than simply refusing to grumble against other people.

With the total context in view, Paul could very well be referring to guarding against an attitude which complains and argues *with God.* Follow the entire thought again. The attitude of Jesus was that of yieldedness to His Father. We are to demonstrate the same attitude that Jesus had as we work out our own salvation with fear and trembling. Now he says, "Do it all without complaining or arguing (with God)." The disposition which is ever prone to "complain and grumble" against God over what He has allowed to happen, either to us or to others, never makes for a spirit of unity with Christ. It dissipates such oneness. Invariably then, that spirit drives to complaining and grumbling and arguing against each other also. And nothing is more uninviting to unsaved people than a grumbling, complaining batch of Christians!

On the contrary, we are to be "blameless and pure, children of God without fault in a crooked and depraved generation." The word "blameless" most likely has to do with how we live before others. Paul is saying that we should live carefully before an onlooking world. The word "pure" has more to do with our inward heart state before God, our motives and thoughts. These are to be kept without guile. The result—God will not fault us, though we are living in a crooked and depraved generation!

But none of this transpires automatically! Paul is informing us that striving to be blameless before men and maintaining pure motives before God both constitute our own personal obligation before God. And obligation calls for accountability! So let us guard our hearts, our motives and our actions carefully as we sincerely endeavor to obey the Lord Jesus Christ.

*PRAYER: Great God we thank You that Jesus has set for us the perfect example of obedience to His heavenly Father. He fulfilled His obligations joyfully. He is our pattern and standard. Help us today to fulfill our duties to You by obeying You as our Lord without complaining or arguing or murmuring or disputing. We ask this in Jesus' name. Amen.*

*WEEK 6: Wednesday*
*READ: Philippians 2:12-18 one more time (focus on verses 15-18)*

## ILLUMINATION FOR GOD

In connection with his theme of obedience, the apostle speaks in today's section of OUR ILLUMINATION FOR GOD. Read verse 15: we are to be "children of God without fault in a crooked and depraved generation," so writes Paul, *"in which you shine like stars in the universe . . ."* The King James rendering is probably better: ". . . among whom ye shine as lights in the world."

The picture he paints is of a world that is darkened by its crooked and depraved condition. Christians who are obediently "working out" their own salvation with fear and trembling become sources of "light which shine in the darkness." In John 8:12 Jesus said, *"I am the light of the world."* And He, by the Holy Spirit, beams His light into your heart and mine—until, in a very real sense, you and I have the light of the world in us! We become His lights as Christ shines out through us in our everyday living and in our countenances. Thus Jesus, speaking to His disciples, was able to truthfully say also in Matthew 5:14, *"You* are the light of the world."

Shortly after I became a Christian, I met a man who I felt knew what it meant to really "let his light shine." Glen was born in the hills of Kentucky, had developed the typical philosophy of a hill farmer, had found Christ, and knew in his heart what it meant to be filled with the Holy Spirit. He used to play his guitar and sing. And he would sing one song with his typical hill twang which I especially recall. It went like this: "Oh, yes, you'll shine—of course, you'll shine! If you really have the blessing, you will shine!" And as he would sing, he would shine! His whole countenance betrayed openly that he loved Jesus Christ with all his heart. He "really had the blessing." And he knew what it meant to "really shine"!

Now what do we learn from our text concerning the illumination of a Christian? Three thoughts. First, we can see *the place for our shining: "in the midst* of a crooked and depraved generation *among whom* ye shine . . ."* The idea is that we enlighten a darkened world. Light is worth nothing unless it shines where the darkness is. So here is not a call to withdraw from all who are "worldly," or to seclude ourselves from "sinners." Jesus did not set that type of a "touch me not" example. He came *into* a world and moved *among* the lost. And you and I, as Christ's representatives in the world, are not to retreat from the dark place. We are to be *in* the world and move *in the midst* of the darkness—*but shine!* The greater the darkness, the brighter will be our light—if we shine!

We can also see *the passion for our shining: ". . .* in which you shine as stars in the world, *as you hold out the word of life."* One of the greatest evidences of the amount of darkness in this world is seen in the fact that people in general are so over-whelmingly ignorant of the Word of God. And it is this word which reveals the Living Word! Let us faithfully hold out the word of life so that others may learn to understand and come to know the Living Word.

Finally, we see *the prize for our shining:* hold out the word of life "in order that *I may boast on the day of Christ that I did not run or labor for nothing.* But even if I am being poured out like a drink offering on the sacrifice and service coming from your faith, I am glad and rejoice with all of you. So you, too, should be glad and rejoice with me." Paul is claiming that if these Christians at Philippi will continue to radiate the true light, such shining will serve as undeniable evidence that Paul's work among them had been genuine. He would not only be able to rejoice here and now, but on that testing day at the judg-ment seat of Christ he will also be glad that he had not run or labored for nothing. On that day, when the Christians' works are judged, Paul says that these saints from Philippi will be there, too. And if he is able to rejoice because they have been genuine shining lights, that would mean they, too, will be able to be joyful.

How then about us? Let us pray God to help us. By His grace let us purpose to be truly shining people _in our world_. As we radiate His presence, others will be able to see and come to the true Light—and we, too, will be able to rejoice on that testing day!

_PRAYER: Lord Jesus Christ, Thou Light of the world, shine upon us today. Illuminate our hearts with the light of heaven that we, too, may glow in the dark and depraved world. May the light of Your presence and the glory of Your grace give us the true power to brighten the hearts of others that they, too, will know what it means to shine. We ask this in Jesus' name. Amen._

┌─────────────────────────────────┐
│                                 │
│  **DEPENDABLE SAINTS** (2:19-30) │
│                                 │
│  **Straightforward Saints (2:19-30)** │
│  **Selfless Saints (2:19-30)**   │
│  **Serving Saints (2:19-30)**    │
│                                 │
└─────────────────────────────────┘

WEEK 6:  Thursday
READ:  Philippians 2:19-30

## DEPENDABLE SAINTS

The theme which we will be considering today, and for the next three days, is not without its underlying inferences. "Dependable saints" suggests, of course, that some saints might not always be so reliable—and that some for that matter, might be quite fickle. In our Scripture lesson, Paul introduces us to two of his co-workers who, whatever their other virtues, were also very trustworthy.

Paul was making plans, at the time of his writing of this epistle, to send both of these men to the Christians at Philippi. He would dispatch each for a different reason. One would be on his way very soon, the other would follow some time later.

Now let us reconstruct the whole scene. The apostle is in prison for his faith. He is not being held, however, in a dungeon type setting. In fact, he is able to live in his own house. But he is chained to a prison guard at all times. He is dictating a letter to the church at Philippi which has sent him a special gift of money. At this point in the letter which forms today's text, he is telling his friends at Philippi of his plans to send these men to them.

The first of whom he speaks is the one he plans to send at a later date. He is Timothy. In the eyes of Paul, he is one of the finest of pastors, and is one of his dearest friends. He speaks of the second in the second section of this reading. This man he plans to send immediately. He is Epaphroditus, who was the messenger who, sometime previously, had brought the gift to Paul from the congregation at Philippi. And he it is who will carry this letter back to the Philippian Christians from Paul. He is a layman.

The outstanding qualities of dependability accorded to these two fellow workers of Paul can be seen in these verses. For the next three days we will consider three marks of their trustworthiness. They were SAINTS WHO WERE STRAIGHTFORWARD, SELFLESS AND SERVING. As we consider the characteristics of these dedicated men, let us be asking God to work into us these marks of dependability that we, too, may be saints who are straightforward, selfless and serving.

*PRAYER: Living Lord of heaven, thank you for the example set by saints who have lived before us. We praise You for the memory of their lives. We are grateful for the record of Timothy and Epaphroditus. We thank You, too, for modern saints who exemplify dependability. Help us this day to be truly reliable. We pray this in Christ's name. Amen.*

*WEEK 6: Friday*
*READ: Philippians 2:19-30 again*

## STRAIGHTFORWARD SAINTS

Timothy and Epaphroditus were STRAIGHTFORWARD

SAINTS! They were open, honest, honorable, above board, forthright and trustworthy!

Take Timothy first—Paul says, "I hope in the Lord Jesus to send Timothy to you soon, that I also may be cheered when I receive news about you." Paul knew Timothy well. From the time he met him on his second missionary journey, a close friendship in Christ had developed. Timothy accompanied him throughout much of his ministry. He was with Paul in Philippi (Acts 16), in Thessalonica and Berea (Acts 17), and in Corinth and Ephesus (Acts 18 & 19). He was by his side in the prison in Rome as seen in Colossians 1:1 and Philippians 1:1.

One of Timothy's specialties in service was to substitute for Paul to various churches. He was the type of person whom Paul could trust to represent him and what he stood for accurately. Thus, when he wished to secure information from one of the churches, or give advice or encouragement or rebuke, if he could not go himself, Paul would send Timothy. He assigned him to go to Thessalonica (I Thess. 3:6), to Corinth (I Cor. 4:17 and 16:10-11), and to Philippi as we read in our text. Apparently, in the hands of Timothy, a message was as safe as if Paul had delivered it himself—he was fully trustworthy! In the end, Timothy himself became a prisoner for Christ's sake as we read in Hebrews 13:23.

We glean something of the same picture when we pick up on the second man of whom Paul writes—Epaphroditus. When the Philippians had heard that Paul was in prison their hearts were moved to send him a gift (probably money). They chose Epaphroditus to deliver this token of love and concern to him. But do you and I realize what it had to mean for this man to be willing to take this contribution to Paul? Paul was being held by Roman authorities on a capital charge which could result in the death penalty. Epaphroditus himself could also be charged with associating with Paul. But he was straightforward enough and sufficiently trustworthy that the Christians at Philippi could well afford to place this gift in his hands. They knew that, in spite of the very real dangers involved, he would come through.

What does Paul have to say about Epaphroditus in our text? He calls him, "My brother, fellow worker and fellow soldier, who was also your messenger, whom you sent to take care of my needs." So he not only delivered the gift, but remained on for a time to minister to Paul's prison needs. And he did this in the face of all the personal peril which accompanied such a ministry.

So here are two men of whom we can say, "They were dependable in that they were straightforward." They were up front people who could be trusted completely, notwithstanding the favorable or unfavorable circumstances. Can we take our lesson? If we are to be counted as dependable people, honesty is a necessity! Someone has said, "The measure of one's true dependability is assessed not by how well he reacts in public, but by how well he performs when no one receives the glory except God." Let us ever strive, by God's help, to be such people.

_PRAYER: Dear Lord Jesus Christ, dependability is so important in Your work. We are sometimes so undependable. Help us to purpose, by the help of Your indwelling Spirit, to so discipline and order our lives that You can count us as trustworthy, reliable people. Grant this request for Jesus' sake. Amen._

## SELFLESS SAINTS

Timothy and Epaphroditus manifested a second mark of dependability. Yesterday we saw that these men were STRAIGHT-FORWARD SAINTS. Today we shall take note of the fact that they were SELFLESS SAINTS—both Timothy and Epaphroditus were genuinely concerned about the affairs of Christ and others before their own interests.

Paul says of Timothy, "I have no one else like him, who takes a genuine interest in your welfare. For everyone looks out for his own interests, not those of Jesus Christ." Apparently Timothy was deeply and genuinely disturbed over the needs of other people—and he took time to minister to those necessities. I cannot read Paul's statement here without feeling forced to pose to myself some disturbing questions. Paul had been surrounded by some other great men also. We know that Luke and Aristarchus had accompanied him to Rome. Mark and Silas had been with him. Yet he says he had no one else like Timothy! Where were these men at this time? Surely they were busy in the work of Christ! But possibly at this particular time they were "too busy" to hear the cry of human need. I have no desire to "second guess" the scriptural statement made here, nor do I want to misrepresent these respectable and faithful companions of Paul. Just who all are embodied in this assertion I am not sure. I do not like to think that Aristarchus or Luke or Mark or Silas would have been "so involved" in their own concerns that they had no time for Paul. But apparently there were some who could have been free to help, but were wrapped up in their "own interests." Timothy saw his need and "took time" to minister.

I fear that most of us must confess at times that much of our time and potential is spent being overly concerned with "our own affairs"—legitimate, necessary cares! Our time fills up with a daily round of demands and responsibilities—and the dire needs of others are completely ignored. May the Lord help us! If we are to be truly dependable to God, we must be willing to allow Him to interrupt our thoughts, cancel our plans, and extend to us new opportunities to help people when and where they hurt. Most of us will struggle if we will be dependable— for the majority of us nurse the notion that our work is so urgent that we cannot afford anything to disturb our plans and schedules. We are totally convinced that we are doing God "a special service" in this practice. We do not want a life that is interrupted!

We see this selfless spirit in Epaphroditus as well. He was genuinely interested in Paul at a time when Paul needed it more than at any other time in his ministry. He was imprisoned, awaiting the outcome, hoping to live, questioning if he might die. Why did Epaphroditus journey from Philippi to Rome to be with Paul? Well, first as we have seen, he came to bring him the offering from the Christians at Philippi. But he also came "to take care of Paul's needs." And while performing this service, Epaphroditus became sick and almost died. But here he was, giving of himself and helping Paul, though he himself was gravely ill. That is dependability!

According to what the apostle writes, God had touched Epaphroditus and spared his life, and now Paul is planning to send him back to Philippi. Lest there should be those at Philippi who might suspicion that Epaphroditus was "walking out on his duty" by leaving Paul, he writes, "Therefore, I am all the more eager to send him, so that when you see him again you may be glad and I may have less anxiety. Welcome him in the Lord with great joy and honor men like him, because he almost died for the work of Christ . . ." He had a selfless spirit! May God help us to strive for the same type of dedication!

*PRAYER: Dear Lord Jesus, we thank You for the privilege of being able to help others. You yourself left us the supreme example. Help us today to put Christ first, others second, and ourselves last. Grant us grace to be selfless Christians, we pray in Jesus' name. Amen.*

———————————◆◆◆——————————

*WEEK 7: Sunday*
*READ: Philippians 2:19-30 one more time*

### SERVING SAINTS

We have seen from this section of Scripture that Timothy and Epaphroditus were STRAIGHTFORWARD SAINTS and SELFLESS SAINTS. Today we will find that they were also SERVING SAINTS. Both were genuinely given to the *work* of the gospel. Paul says of Timothy that he "proved himself, because as a son with his father he has served with me in the work of the gospel." Timothy not only loved Jesus Christ, but he also served Him! And what does he say about Epaphroditus? He calls him his "fellow worker" and "fellow soldier." He says he "almost died for the work of Christ, risking his life to make up for the help you (Philippians) could not give me."

From the two epistles Paul wrote to Timothy, we can conclude unquestionably that this young man was a rather introverted and withdrawn soul. He was probably quiet, even delicate, and a rather sickly type of person. Paul found it necessary to encourage him often not to be ashamed and not to let anyone despise his youth. He urged him to be strong, to take care of his stomach and guard against his many infirmities. On the other hand, according to what Paul says here, Epaphroditus was just the opposite—he "risked his life" for Paul. The original word is actually one of abandon, the word used literally for "gambling," as when one "threw dice." Apparently he was a rather "reckless" type of Christian. He was one who, though he had become desperately ill even unto death in the work of Christ, just kept pellmelling his way along! He was a "risk it all" type of man who was willing to throw himself into the labor God had given him to do, willing to gamble his very life for the cause of Christ!

Now here is the lesson. We observe two extremely opposite types of personalities, *both* of whom God was using in His work of ministering. Oh, yes—God marvelously used them both! Each exercised faithfully the gifts the Spirit had given him. Each served Jesus Christ in an effective way in the power of the Holy Spirit sent down from heaven. Neither mimicked the other. Each was deeply dedicated to working for the Savior.

And we may be sure that God is still ferreting out a multiplicity of personalities today! He is seeking all kinds of individuals who represent every type of temperament. And He will press into His service all who are willing. To reason, "I can't serve God—I'm too quiet and introverted," simply cannot be acceptable. Timothy was also quite shy and sensitive, and God used him in a surprising way. To say, "I am just too foolhardy by nature—God can't use me," is just as unacceptable. Epaphroditus also possessed a rather adventuresome spirit, and God used him! God wants you just as you are, totally yielded to Him! If you are submitted to God and willing to serve, He will utilize your abilities. But He is not interested in using you as He operates with another. You are the only you that God has created— you simply cannot be anyone else! Let God use you according to the gifts He has invested in you. There is absolutely no *need* to copy-cat anyone else, for it is *you* God wants to employ in His service!

Here are two men in our text whose personalities were radically different from each other, but both were extremely dependable. They were straightforward. They were selfless. They were serving. May we draw on God's grace to "go and do likewise."

*PRAYER: Dear Master in heaven, we are Your servants. You want to use us in Your work. You have given gifts to Your people, and have invested at least one in each of us. Help us to recognize our gift or gifts, and be willing to exercise those God-given abilities under the enabling power of the Spirit of God, in a yielded way, in the work of God. We ask this in Jesus Christ's name. Amen.*

---

### IN WHAT IS YOUR CONFIDENCE? (3:1-3)

**A Word of Adulation (3:1)**
**A Word of Admonition (3:2)**
**A Word of Affirmation (3:3)**

*WEEK 7: Monday*
*READ: Philippians 3:1-3*

### IN WHAT IS YOUR CONFIDENCE?

Entering chapter three in our study of this letter, we discover that the accent of what Paul writes suddenly changes. To this point he has basically done two things—he has shared his own inner feelings concerning his prison posture, rejoicing that the gospel is being advanced through such unwelcome circumstances. And he has urged the Philippians to follow the example of Christ's yieldedness and humility. Coming through chapters one and two we have sensed no negative overtones. He has expressed his positive appreciation for the Christians at Philippi and has given special tribute to Timothy and Epaphroditus.

In chapter three, however, this positive tone fades and his emphasis turns to that of warning. And his mood takes on a negative air—even to the point of sarcasm. His anxiety is agitated by false teachers in the church and their counterfeit doctrines.

In order that we might more fully appreciate both what Paul has written here and the spirit he displays in his assertion, it is very important to keep a clearly defined backdrop in our total picture. He was writing, as with all his epistles, during a time of transition. The Holy Spirit was ushering the church into the day of grace. As was true of most of the first Christians, Paul had been converted to Christ while _in_ Judiasm. His about-face had taken place from a very legalistic background in the Mosaic law. Under such law, acceptance by God was conditioned upon "fully obeying that law" with all of its ceremonies and ritual. Since coming to know Christ, Paul's entire concept had been radically altered. He had come to experience and appreciate God's unremunerated grace. He now taught that salvation was a free gift, that it could not be earned through performing the letter of the law—only lovingly accepted by faith in Christ! He taught that God offered this salvation to _both_ Jews and Gentiles on this basis—none were excluded!

It is not surprising then that many found it difficult to embrace the idea that one could be "saved by grace alone." Wherever Paul taught free grace, others countered by maintaining that no one could be saved apart from fulfilling the ritual of the law (especially the practice of the rite of circumcision). These teachers who fostered the countless deeds of the law followed him like blood hounds and persistently endeavored to undermine his teaching. They called themselves Christians and propagated the concept that only Jews could be saved, and that if Gentiles desired salvation in Christ they must come under this aspect of the law which called for circumcision.

Paul's reaction to such indoctrination, and to those who taught it, was caustic! And his mental stance, as we shall see, betrays itself openly in this section. For the next three days we will consider what he had to say concerning this untruthful teaching and his correction of the same. On Tuesday we will look into HIS WORD OF ADULATION, on Wednesday, HIS WORD OF ADMONITION, and Thursday, HIS WORD OF AFFIRMATION. As we study we must ask ourselves in all honesty, "In what have we placed our confidence for salvation?" In our own works? Or in the grace of God? May the Holy Spirit teach us how to fully trust Christ and Christ alone, for salvation and keeping grace.

*PRAYER: Dear Father of our Lord Jesus Christ, Author of grace and truth, grant us clear understanding as we study this short section of this Philippian letter for the next three days. We want to be able to fully appreciate the wonderful everlasting grace of our Lord Jesus Christ, in whose name we pray. Amen.*

WEEK 7: Tuesday
READ: Philippians 3:1-3 again (look at verse 1)

## A WORD OF ADULATION

Before Paul actually becomes involved in his rather sarcastic reaction to the false teaching of salvation by works which was being propagated in his day, he gives vent, first, to A WORD OF ADULATION. In verse 1 we read, "Finally, my brothers, rejoice in the Lord . . ." Stop there for now. This, of course, is not the first time in this epistle that Paul has called on the Philippian Christians, and all Christians, to be rejoicing people. In fact, he has exhorted us to "rejoice" or to "be joyful" or to "be glad" five times thus far—and before he finishes the letter he will ask us two more times to "rejoice in the Lord always"! Add to this the fact that he also has stated on five occasions previous to this section that he himself was "being joyful" or "rejoicing" and before he closes the epistle he will declare twice more that he is "greatly rejoicing" and "has joy." That totals fifteen times in this prison letter that he speaks of being joyful. Further, if we include such words as "praise," "praiseworthy," "thanks," "glory," "cheer," etc., we would yet find seven more times that he expresses this positive attitude of exuberance in the Lord.

No wonder he makes the statement that he does in our text: "It is no trouble for me to write the same things to you again . . ." —i.e. I have already said it in this short letter a number of times, but I don't mind repeating it again—"Rejoice!"

But note the stipulation he places on that rejoicing: "Rejoice *in the Lord.*" Circumstances may not always set a proper stage for being joyful. But the trusting child of God can afford to rejoice anyway, for his joy is not hinged on circumstances, but centers rather *in the Lord!*

While pastoring in Marshall, Michigan, my wife and I were privileged to become acquainted with a very remarkable example of this type of rejoicing. The mother of one of the members of the church lived in a nearby town. She was outstanding—a shining, Godly, victorious Christian! She had formed the habit of being joyous in her Savior. One day we received word through her son that Mrs. Schrock's doctor had discovered that she had contracted cancer of the bone. The news greatly shocked all of us! With other Christians in a number of churches, we helped beseech God for her healing. And for a period of time she did, in fact, show signs of improvement, and all who were praying were greatly encouraged.

Then came word that the malignant condition had worsened. My wife and I visited her, hopeful of encouraging her. But the surprise was ours! Her spirit was still buoyant. Her faith was positive. Her smile was genuine. Her joy in Christ was effervescent. All of this in spite of the fact that she carried her arm in a sling for the bone had become weakened sufficiently that it could not support the weight. She joked about her "sympathy sling," and told us how much she loved Jesus. She laughed and talked about heaven. I have never met anyone who was able to rejoice more in the midst of such intense suffering than did Mrs. Schrock!

In time she passed away. But no one could be sad. Her attitude while she lived would not permit us to think negative thoughts at the time of her funeral. She had learned to "rejoice in the Lord always." In spite of all of her desperate circumstances, she died triumphantly—and shall ever be remembered as one joyful Christian!

And why be a rejoicing Christian? There are a number of motivating factors, of course! Paul states one of those reasons here. He says that we should rejoice because "it is a safeguard for you." Oh yes! It is ever safe to rejoice in the Lord always! On the other hand, the opposite attitude of allowing discouragement to rule one's heart is always spiritually dangerous. So let us evermore be about the business of "rejoicing in the Lord." It will help guard us against the danger about which Paul will warn us in the next few lines. Thank God for this WORD OF ADULATION!

*PRAYER: Blessed Lord Jesus, happiness always tends to make us positive people. We have many reasons to rejoice in You. You have given us salvation. You have provided for our physical, emotional and spiritual needs. You have given us the possibility of a useful life and the hope of heaven. Help us ever to rejoice in these mercies. Grant that this day will be a joyful day in Christ. Amen.*

---

WEEK 7: Wednesday
READ: Philippians 3:1-3 again (consider verse 2)

## A WORD OF ADMONITION

Yesterday we considered Paul's WORD OF ADULATION. Now today in verse 2 he expresses his WORD OF ADMONITION: "Watch out for (beware of) those dogs, those men who do evil, those mutilators of the flesh." Do you feel the sarcasm oozing from his pen in this warning statement?

As the context reveals, this strikingly terse admonition is thrown out concerning the false teachers and their counterfeit indoctrination, which greatly troubled Paul in his ministry. These self-appointed instructors tenaciously insisted that none could be saved by Christ through grace alone, but rather all must be saved by "trusting Christ and submitting to the ritual and ceremonies of the Mosaic law."

Now let us take particular note of the very marked difference between Paul's attitude here and his much more tolerant frame of mind displayed in chapter 1, verses 15-18. There he spoke of those who preach the true gospel but with wrong motives. His feeling was, "What does it matter? The important thing is that in every way, whether from false motive or true, Christ is preached and because of this I rejoice." Here his attitude is completely the opposite: "Watch out for those dogs, those men who are evil, those mutilators of the flesh."

Why the difference? In the first instance, though the motives were wrong, the message and representation of Christ was true. In this second instance, not only were the motives erroneous, but they also completely misrepresented the person and message of Jesus Christ. The first band of teachers was at least maintaining that salvation was possible through the grace of God by faith in Christ alone. The second were, in effect, ruling Christ out as the only Savior by maintaining that salvation was possible only by the works of the law. That was a complete misrepresentation of the work of Christ—and that Paul could not and would not tolerate!

So he warns, "Beware of those dogs . . ." And in our text, Paul is basically alluding to the parial dogs, scavengers which roamed the streets, hunting amidst garbage dumps, feeding on the refuse and filth of the alleys. Does Paul sound cruel? Take note also that it ·vas not only the teachings, but also the works of these men which stirred Paul's indignation—"Watch out for those dogs, *those men who do evil* . . ." He is addressing himself to the issues involved in the teachings of those who were trying to earn their salvation by their good works. Let us not misunderstand Paul here. He is not decrying the fact that they desired to perform works, but rather that they expected to be saved by those works! Catch Paul's insinuation then—when good works are performed with the motive of earning salvation by the merits of those works, in God's sight, those very good works become evil!

Now let us update what Paul is saying. Consider the ritual and ceremonies of the Christian church. When one trusts his baptism, for instance, as the means of salvation rather than recognizing it as a symbolic testimony of inner cleansing by faith, that very baptism, which is good, becomes to him a very deceiving type of evil work. We might say the same concerning church membership, the observance of communion, living righteous lives, tithing, saying prayers, reading the Bible, church attendance and on and on! None of these is a means of salvation, but rather the results of and witness to our salvation, which is received by faith alone.

Finally he says, "Watch out for . . . those mutilators of the flesh." Here again Paul writes with a sarcastic pen! He is signaling out what was considered one of the most important religious practices of his day, and one which these teachers claimed was necessary for salvation—the rite of circumcision, inherited from Judiasm. These false teachers were demanding circumcision of all who professed Christ, declaring that those who refused certainly could not be accepted by God as *true* Christians. Paul mocks that false concept of spirituality. He maintains that, in such a case, where their dependence is on circumcision for salvation, all that has actually resulted is that they have mutilated their flesh, to no spiritual advantage at all!

Are you prone to feel that Paul did not demonstrate a very noble Christian spirit by utilizing such cutting and blunt responses concerning these teachers and their false doctrine? After all, he could have disagreed without being sarcastic. But recognize clearly, he is dealing with a teaching which completely undermined the very work of Christ! To follow such instruction would cause one to fall short of actually receiving salvation. And to miss the mark at that point is not only to miss true teaching, but to miss heaven! And to miss heaven is to miss it all! We can learn a lesson here. When a teaching is being put forth which will cause one to miss heaven, there can be little doubt that the most noble and most Christian reaction we can offer is to bluntly speak out against is, no holds barred! That is what Paul does here—A WORD OF ADMONITION!

*PRAYER: Thou eternal Author of faith, our salvation is in You and You alone. We bring nothing to You that merits salvation. We claim nothing except the fact that Jesus died for us. Thank You for Your work on the cross. It is enough! We trust You fully. Grant us grace to express that faith by our lives this day, in Christ's name. Amen.*

WEEK 7:  *Thursday*
READ:  *Philippians 3:1-3 one final time (reread verse 3)*

## A WORD OF AFFIRMATION

In what is your confidence for salvation? In your good works? Or is it placed solely in Christ? In the three verses of today's reading Paul helps us to understand clearly in whom our confidence should be placed. We must trust Christ alone for our salvation! He has given us an incentive to "rejoice in the Lord" (A WORD OF ADULATION). He has warned against those who insist that we must be saved, at least to some degree, by our works rather than by faith in Christ (A WORD OF AD-MONITION). Now today we will hear HIS WORD OF AF-FIRMATION. In verse 3 he says, "For it is we who are the circumcision . . ." And he proceeds then to describe his intent by such a statement in this context—and what becomes very transparent is that we have a right to glory only in Christ Jesus, and in nothing else!

Misguided teachers of Paul's day made great issue of the necessity of participating in the rite of circumcision of the flesh before one could be saved. And Paul has vehemently contra-dicted such a false concept by asserting that if one is bent on trusting such a ritual for salvation, it amounts to nothing more than mutilating the flesh!

On the other hand, according to Colossians 2:11-13, there is a spiritual circumcision so designed that sin may be cut away—and Paul claims in our text that this is the type of circumcision that really counts. In verse 3, with three brief descriptive phrases, he relates what is involved in this kind of spiritual re-lationship with God.

First he says, "For it is we who are the circumcision, we who worship by the Spirit of God . . ." Paul affirms this, as opposed to the argument that the only way God may be worshipped is through the ritualism and legalities of the Mosaic law. True worship and a vital relationship with Jesus Christ penetrates much deeper than ceremonies. These result from being born of the Spirit and filled with the Spirit—they flow out of a life that is totally yielded to the Holy Spirit.

So we "worship by the Spirit of God," and are among those "who glory in Christ Jesus"—and the inference is that we glory in nothing else and no one else except Christ! Jesus himself offers a real life illustration of this very point. He said two men went to the temple to pray. The first, a religious Pharisee, stood and prayed, "God, I thank you that I am not like all other men—robbers, evildoers, adulterers—or even like this tax collector. I fast twice a week and give a tenth of all my income." The publican did not so much as lift his eyes to heaven, but beat his breast and prayed, "God, have mercy on me, a sinner!" Jesus said, "I tell you that this man, rather than the other, went home justified before God" (Luke 18:9-14). The first gloated in all that he did and did not do—and what he did and did not do was very commendable! But Paul protests! That is not the point around which our glorying should rally! After all, we have no legitimate reason whatever to boast concerning what we do and do not do as Christians—for when we have done all, "we are unworthy servants; we have only done our duty" (Luke 17:10). Where is our glory and boasting then? "We glory in Christ Jesus," who has saved us by His mercy alone. We are nothing more than sinners saved by grace! All of the praise and the honor be to Jesus Christ our Savior and our Lord!

And besides all this, Paul adds that we "put no confidence in the flesh." The sum total of our confidence rests completely in the work of Christ on the cross, not in our own works without the cross! Our hope of salvation and heaven is firmly grounded in what Christ has done for us—not in what we have done for Him!

Let you and I ask ourselves anew, "In whom or what is my confidence focused?" Are we quite confident that we are going to go to heaven because we attend church, are honest, and do not do a lot of questionable things? Let us be reminded that our safety is not found there. Our safety is found in trusting Christ alone!

*PRAYER: Jesus Christ, Son of the living God, we thank You for the privilege of anchoring our faith in You and You alone. Grant us Your grace to walk by faith and to live to Your honor and glory in that faith. May our boasting be in Jesus, in whose name we pray. Amen.*

```
┌─────────────────────────────────────────────────┐
│                                                   │
│   COUNTING ALL BUT LOSS FOR CHRIST (3:4-11)      │
│                                                   │
│   Counting Personal Gain but Loss (3:4-8)        │
│   Counting Penitential Loss All Gain (3:8-9)     │
│   Counting on Perpetual Gain from Loss (3:10-11) │
│                                                   │
└─────────────────────────────────────────────────┘
```

*WEEK 7: Friday*
*READ: Philippians 3:4-11*

## COUNTING ALL BUT LOSS FOR CHRIST

The freedom banner which the Apostle Paul waved victoriously before the world of his day declared full and free salvation for all men everywhere! He pressed tenaciously for the truth that this gift of complete salvation was made effective in the hearts of individuals through the work of Jesus Christ by faith in Him alone—not by the works of the law. But many religious teachers in his day, as in ours, were convinced that faith in Christ alone was not sufficient to save. They insisted that the performance of the works of the ritual of the law was also necessary if one was to realize such salvation. Simply stated, their theology perceived that sinners were made right before God by faith and the works of the law.

In the context preceding today's section, you will remember, Paul has warned his readers in a very terse way to "watch out for those dogs" who taught such false doctrine, calling them "men who do evil" and "mutilators of the flesh." He has given us to understand that true worship is that which is "by the Spirit of God" and is performed by those who only "glory in Christ Jesus" and who "put no confidence in the flesh."

For us to be able to intelligently comprehend the scope of Paul's teaching we must update the principles and apply them to our present set of circumstances. When one assumes, for instance, that for a lost sinner to become a Christian, he must not only turn from his sins and trust Christ, but also be baptized, join a church, and receive communion, he is presuming precisely what Paul condemns here. Or when one teaches that a seeker after God must first straighten out his past and prove he can live a good life before he can be saved, he again is demanding what Paul here condemns. To affirm that we are saved by faith *plus* the performance of any type of good work is to cut into the core of the very issue Paul counterblows. If one must be saved by his works at all, to that degree it must become necessary to place confidence, not only in Christ, but also in the flesh, in order to be counted right before God. That is precisely what Paul denies in our text!

Paul has stated clearly that our glory is "in Christ Jesus" alone and that we must "put no confidence in the flesh." He now sets out in today's text to further establish those facts by giving his own testimony as to how he came to know Christ Jesus. Tomorrow we will consider how he COUNTED PERSONAL GAIN BUT LOSS. On Sunday we will find how he COUNTED PENITENTIAL LOSS ALL GAIN, and on Monday how he COUNTED ON PERPETUAL GAIN FROM LOSS. Or we might say that he speaks of renunciation, reconciliation and resurrection. Let us keep our hearts and minds open to God's Spirit as we study together this very personal section involving Paul's relationship with Jesus Christ.

*PRAYER: Dear Father in heaven, we thank You for the adequate provision You have put into effect for us through Your Son Jesus Christ. Teach us to understand more and more what it means to "count all but loss for Christ." Grant us the grace to live out that attitude, placing all of our confidence in Christ alone. Guard us from putting any confidence in the flesh and we shall praise You in Jesus' name. Amen.*

## COUNTING PERSONAL GAIN BUT LOSS

Today we will note how Paul COUNTED PERSONAL GAIN BUT LOSS—that is renunciation! He said in verse 3, as we have seen previously, that we should "put no confidence in the flesh." Now, in today's text, he continues, "Though I myself have reasons for such confidence, if anyone else thinks he has reason to put confidence in the flesh, I have more." Paraphrased, he is saying, "We cannot be saved by our works—but if we could, I would be a more likely candidate than anyone else." And he enumerates some of his "good works" which of certainty would have counted as "personal gain" if such works could save. These included his ancestry, his orthodoxy, his activity and his morality. And his claim is that, if one could pile up points with God, in all four of these categories his score would have excelled!

It arouses my curiosity that anyone should presume to gloat in his *ancestry*—after all, he had very little to do with it! But Paul boasts, "If ancestry counts, look at mine! Proper ritual and proper birth are both in order—circumcised on the eighth day, of the people of Israel, of the tribe of Benjamin, a Hebrew of the Hebrews!" He was a pure blooded Israelite (not part Gentile)— both mother and father were undiluted Hebrews!

And what about *orthodoxy?* Paul flaunts the fact that he belonged to the most orthodox of the Jewish structure (a Pharisee not a Saducee). He could also have added that he was the son of a Pharisee (Acts 23:6). That is the equivalent to saying, "I am a fundamentalist and the son of a fundamentalist!" It is like affirming, "I am a conservative of the conservatives!" If such orthodoxy in itself could be sufficient to get one to heaven, salvation would be unnecessary! The only issue would be to "join the right church."

And Paul's *activity* for the sake of what he believed would be hard to beat! He says, "As for zeal, persecuting the church!" He invested more effort and drive and work into what he believed than most Christians do into what they believe! And he did it all sincerely! He was convinced that he was doing God service!

And look at his *morality:* "As for legalistic righteousness, faultless!" He had disciplined himself to perform all of the legal "do's and don'ts" of the law. No one could fault his moral be havior. It is nothing but commendable. Do you feel that you have "lived a good life"? Are you satisfied that you have obeyed all of the "Ten Commandments"? So did Paul—probably with more sincerity than any of us.

But what was Paul's attitude toward all of this? his ancestry? his orthodoxy? his activity? his morality? One might suppose that he would amass it together and build it all into strong arguments why God should accept him into heaven! That is precisely what many religious people are doing today. Desperately hoping to earn their way to heaven by their "good lives" and their "religious activities," they have quite confidently concluded that God simply could not be God and allow someone as fine as themselves to be lost.

Was this Paul's attitude? Read his words: "But whatever was to my profit I now consider loss for the sake of Christ. What is more, I consider everything a loss compared to the surpassing greatness of knowing Christ Jesus my Lord, for whose sake I have lost all things. I consider them rubbish that I may gain Christ . . ." Paul reckoned all of those good things that could be stated of him as nothing but loss! So far as being a means of salvation, he renounced it all! None of it could save!

So Paul, first of all, counted personal gain but loss. That is renunciation. And what was necessary for Paul is necessary for us. Let us recognize clearly that all of our righteousness and all of our good works will not save! They will not bring us into a relationship with Christ. We come to know Christ by faith in His sacrifice alone. Let us purpose to trust Him anew today for our salvation.

*JOY IN A ROMAN JAIL*                                          *113*

*PRAYER: Living, resurrected Lord, we thank You for Your wonderful work on Calvary. We thank You for salvation through Your death on the cross and through the power of Your resurrection. We renounce all of our goodness as a means of salvation and we reiterate this day that our faith is in You alone! Help us to consciously and continually count all of our righteousness but loss that we might truly know Christ. We pray this in Your name. Amen.*

WEEK 8: *Sunday*
READ: *Philippians 3:4-11 (focus on verses 8 and 9)*

## COUNTING PENITENTIAL LOSS ALL GAIN

Yesterday we examined how Paul COUNTED PERSONAL GAIN BUT LOSS. We observed his renunciation. Today we will see how he COUNTED PENITENTIAL LOSS ALL GAIN —that is reconciliation! We read in verse 8b the following: "I consider them (all of his good works) rubbish, *that I may gain Christ . . .*"

When Paul speaks here of "gaining Christ" he is not referring to that type of reconciliation which takes place just at conversion—though his thought is, of necessity, built on that foundation. Keep in mind that Paul initially penned these words as one *who had already become a Christian.* He has said in our context that everything he could think of that he might have counted as gain to himself (as a Christian) he had chosen to reckon as loss!

He counted it all loss, he says, "compared to the surpassing greatness of knowing Christ Jesus my Lord." So it seems quite clear that he is referring primarily to the idea of *continually* counting all loss and becoming more and more reconciled to who and what Jesus really is.

In our text he refers to that growing relationship with Christ by two expressions: "the surpassing greatness of knowing Christ" and "gaining Christ." That is, we may come to know Christ in an ever deepening and more meaningful way! And we may be gaining more and more Christlikeness day by day!

We are all very much aware that among the most sincere and dedicated Christians, who at the point of conversion counted all but loss for Christ, can be found personality traits and mental attitudes which are not as much like Christ as they ought to be. Such shortcomings only demonstrate that we need more and more Christlikeness! D.L. Moody was probably one of the most consecreated and Spirit-filled men of his day. And yet Moody was honest enough to state openly, "I've had more trouble with D.L. Moody than with any other man I know."[1] A less sincere man could not afford to confess such.

I have taken special cognizance through the years of the fact that some of the finest "on fire" Christians I have known personally have been those who have never been totally satisfied with their own spiritual attainments. They have never quite been able to be what they really wanted to be spiritually for their goals have always been higher than present attainments! They have been honest enough to confess that fact and were genuinely striving to be more and more like Jesus. These are they who have had the most lasting and effective influence on my life for good! And I must confess that those who have tended to turn me cold, spiritually, have been

[1]From *A Treasury of Sermon Illustrations* edited by Charles L. Wallis. Copyright renewal © 1978 by Charles L. Wallis, p. 254. Used by permission of the publishers, Abingdon Press.

those who have held themselves at a "safe distance" from others. They have never allowed their brothers in Christ to get "too close to them," lest they be discovered to betray one of their weaknesses. They have displayed their holiness on their spiritual shirt sleeves. They have desperately desired that their fellow Christians be sure to notice their spiritual growth. That type of holiness runs so thin!

How does one truly "gain" or "acquire" more and more Christ-likeness? It is certainly not procured by flaunting the progress he has already made in grace! Such increasing holiness is gained rather by continually counting the righteousness which has resulted from such previous progress as nothing, so far as making him *worthy* of God's multiplied grace. One of the most distasteful attitudes a Christian may be tempted to betray is that of becoming smug in his holiness. There were numerous things which Paul did and did not do as a Christian. But what was his attitude toward such goodness? Verses 8 and 9 let us know: "I consider them rubbish, that I might gain Christ, and be found in him, not having a righteousness of my own that comes from the law, but that which is through faith in Christ—the righteousness that comes from God and is by faith."

The basic difference between this type of righteousness and that which tends to drive one to "feel and display" his holiness in a self-righteous way is clear. The first springs from simple faith in Christ and is motivated by a genuine desire that only He be glorified. The other springs from religious pride and is motivated by a desire to draw attention to one's self!

Let us understand very clearly, we will never be able to grow enough spiritually to earn the right to feel that, because we have arrived at such an advanced stage in grace, God owes us heaven! Growth in grace does not make us meritorious of His good favor. We will never *merit* anything from God! All that we have and all that we are have been the result of grace alone! So Paul says, "I consider everything a loss compared to the surpassing greatness of knowing Christ Jesus my Lord." He counted penitential loss all gain—that is reconciliation! Praise His name!

_PRAYER: Dear Father in heaven, thank you for the privilege of knowing Your Son Jesus through grace alone. And in knowing Your Son, we know You. Give us grace to demonstrate the type of righteousness which will simply glorify Him and we will praise You in the name of Jesus our Lord. Amen._

_WEEK 8: Monday_
_READ: Philippians 3:4-11 (consider especially verses 10 and 11)_

## COUNTING ON PERPETUAL GAIN FROM LOSS

For the past two days we have given thought to how Paul COUNTED PERSONAL GAIN BUT LOSS (that is renunciation) and how he COUNTED PENITENTIAL LOSS ALL GAIN (that is reconciliation). Today we will see how he COUNTED ON PERPETUAL GAIN FROM LOSS—that is resurrection! Verses 10 and 11 tell us, "I want to know Christ and the power of His resurrection and the fellowship of sharing in His sufferings, becoming like Him in His death, and so somehow, to attain to the resurrection from the dead." The literal rendering of that last phrase is this: "And so, somehow, to attain to the 'out resurrection' from the dead," or "the resurrection out from the dead." It speaks of a resurrection out from among those who are dead.

The Bible teaches that the next _great_ event on God's divine agenda is the return of Christ in the clouds. The bodies of all who have died in faith will rise from the dead by the power of the resurrection—they will be resurrected out from the dead.

According to Revelation 20:5, the rest of the dead (i.e. those who died outside of faith) will not be resurrected until after a thousand years of the triumphant reign of Christ on earth have transpired. Thus the Bible clearly refers to at least two separate phases of the resurrection—the first, of those who have died in Christ, and the second, of those who have died outside of Christ.

In today's text, we see Paul's final goal. He not only counted everything loss that he might more and more acquire the nature and characteristics of Jesus and come to know Him better and better. He also had his eye focused on the future. For what purpose? That he might be a part of those who will be resurrected out from among the dead in the first resurrection, the resurrection of the saved! He knew that those who will miss this resurrection will be raised again at the resurrection of the lost.

Two other sections in Paul's writings have been given to this theme of the "out resurrection" more minutely and at more length—I Corinthians 15 and I Thessalonians 4 and 5. In both of those epistles, he couples this phase of the resurrection with the rapture, the snatching away of the believers who will be living at the time of His coming. We read that not everyone is going to die, but every believer will be changed, in a moment, in a twinkling of an eye, at the blast of the last trumpet. The dead in Christ will rise first. Then all who are alive and remain will be caught up together with them in the clouds to meet the Lord in the air. From that time on the redeemed will be forever with the Lord! That is the hope of all who are "in faith." Our attitude ought to be that of "looking up" with expectation, longing for His return! Would it not be tremendous to be alive when Jesus returns?

Until then let us continue, as did Paul, to consider all that might be thought of as "gain" in our eyes as loss for the overwhelming greatness of knowing Christ better and better so that we, too, may be a part of that "out resurrection," which time is surely coming.

*PRAYER: Dear Lord Jesus Christ, our present Assurance and our future Hope, we want to be a part of that "first resurrection" when all of Your people, living and dead, shall be caught up to be with You in the air. Thank you for such a tremendous hope! Help us to live with an expectant attitude, ever looking up, knowing that our redemption is drawing nigh. We praise You for the assurance of such a marvelous future. Help us to walk in that hope today. Amen.*

---

## KNOWING CHRIST (3:10)

**Three Methods of Knowing Christ (3:10)**
**Three Marks of Knowing Christ (3:10)**
**Three Measures of Knowing Christ (3:10)**

---

*WEEK 8: Tuesday*
*READ: Philippians 3:10*

## KNOWING CHRIST

One of the most important issues with which we will ever come to grips is bundled up in the question, "What does it mean to know Jesus Christ?" Most of this entire chapter consists of a simple, straightforward testimony on the part of Paul portraying his relationship with Christ and what it meant to him to know the Messiah in a personal way. This theme is so important that I want us to take the next three days to study one verse, verse 10. In this verse, we can come to distinguish Paul's concept of what is involved in "knowing Christ."

In verses 4 through 6, we heard Paul state seven facts about his former life before he became a follower of Christ, maintaining that if anyone ever possessed a claim to salvation through the merits of his own works, he did! But we also heard him renounce that claim, choosing rather to count all that he could have justified as personal gain as loss. This he did for one reason—that he might know Christ!

It is shocking to some people to hear anyone dare to claim, "I know Christ." That self-conceited statement simply has to be presumption in religious garb! Who can dare be so pompous as to assume that he knows Christ! And yet this is precisely the very heart and core of what Paul is asserting in these verses— "I want to know Christ . . ." And we cannot read what he writes without catching the signal that "knowing Christ" is a very real personal experience which is possible for everyone! We get the very practical feeling that Paul was convinced that we can know Christ in such an experiential way that He would be as real to us as any other person. We cannot help but sense that, to Paul, Christ was as real as Barnabas or Timothy! He could not see Christ, but he could know Him!

So the persistent question reasserts itself: "What does it mean, in fact, to know Jesus Christ?" For the next three days we will consider this query. Tomorrow we will study THREE METHODS OF KNOWING CHRIST. On Thursday, we will consider THREE MARKS OF KNOWING CHRIST. And on Friday, we will see THREE MEASURES OF KNOWING CHRIST. Let us ask the Holy Spirit to be our helper as we contemplate these life changing issues.

*PRAYER: Dear Lord Jesus Christ, as Paul expresses in our text, we want to really know You. We want to know what it means to know You in an ever increasing and deepening way. Help us as we study to keep our hearts open so that the knowledge of Christ will become more and more real to our inner hearts. Grant us the joy of being able, with all honesty, to say "we know Jesus."We ask this in His name and for His glory. Amen.*

---

WEEK 8:  *Wednesday*
READ:  *Philippians 3:10*

### THREE METHODS OF KNOWING CHRIST

There are three ways of knowing anything. And we may assert that there are THREE METHODS OF KNOWING CHRIST. First, we may know Him *by inference*—that is, by the exercise of one's power to reason. This method begins with a known fact, adds a middle premise, and formulates a conclusion. Here is an example. Begin with a known fact: "God loves all human beings." Add a middle premise: "I am a human being." Conclusion: "Therefore, God loves me." This procedure, of course, can become extremely complicated. One may commence with a *number* of simple accepted truths, affix many premises, and arrive at a myriad of dependable conclusions. This is not a very warm method of developing knowledge—it is rather "lawyer-like"—but it does result in "knowing."

This is the mode which many have utilized to frame everything they know about Christ. They have read, listened to others and reasoned—and they have contrived certain conclusions. That is the extent of all they know of Christ! Others have pressed further. They have read the Word of God and its promises. One such promise is Romans 10:9: ". . . if you confess with your mouth, 'Jesus is Lord,' and believe in your heart that God raised him from the dead, you will be saved." They reason, "I have confessed with my mouth that Jesus is Lord. I have believed in my heart that God has raised Him from the dead. Therefore, I conclude that I am saved." And if that faith is genuine, such knowledge does, in fact, result. But if it goes no deeper—if there is no witness of God's Holy Spirit to the inner soul—such a knowledge of Christ can be very "heady." It may never vibrate in the soul with any conviction.

Then again, we may acquire knowledge *through our sensibilities*—knowledge which results from what one sees, hears, feels, smells and tastes. Some would call this knowledge by acquaintance. Such "knowing" has more to do with physical experience as opposed to intellectual experience. How does one depict a sunset to a man born blind? Or how can one create the sounds of a symphony to one born deaf? Again, how can one share the marvels of New York City or Chicago to a 10-year-old boy in Africa? In each instance, the person involved must see and feel and hear and taste and smell, or he will never know!

And so a man says, "I never saw Christ. I never heard Him. I never touched or felt Him. How can I know Him?" And that question is valid, for Christ is not now with us in His bodily presence! On the other hand, the song says, "There are some things I may not know; there are some places I can't go, but I am sure of this one thing: that God is real for I can feel Him deep within."[1] We may "see" Him with the eye of faith and "hear" the voice of God in the soul. We are able to "touch" Him in prayer. And all such exercise of our spiritual capacities

---

[1] "My God is Real" by Kenneth Morris. Copyright © 1944 by Hill and Range Songs, Inc. Copyright Renewed, assigned to Unichappell Music, Inc. (Rightsong Music, Publisher). International Copyright Secured. ALL RIGHTS RESERVED. Used by permission.

results in knowledge!

But thirdly, there is knowledge *by awareness*—this is primarily the type of knowledge of which Paul speaks in our text. Such "knowing" can be very practical and real! For example, how do you know that you are who you are? Do you brace up on the edge of your bed every morning and reason it out? Do you listen to your voice, touch your arm and look at your hand and take a view in the mirror and conclude, "Yes sir, I'm still me"? Not at all! You are simply *aware* of the fact that, though your physical body is changing constantly, you are still you! Such inner knowledge gives you much assurance and security.

And I declare that God, by the inner witness of His Holy Spirit, is able to effect in you an *awareness* of the inner presence of His Son in your heart. You may not be able to intellectually rationalize all of the intricate details concerning Him—you will probably not see visions or hear voices—you might not even feel as you desire to feel sometimes. But the Holy Spirit can make you clearly aware of the presence of Christ in you!

How is such a knowledge of His presence generated in us? Well, by all three methods, actually. We must, first, fully accept what is written in God's Word about us and about Christ. His Word reveals that, apart from Him, we are sinful and lost. It affirms that we are in dire need of an inner heart-change. It further calls for repentance and faith, promising salvation to all who believe. We may conclude, therefore, that if we repent truly and believe implicitly God will be faithful to His Word. He will save us! *That is knowledge by inference.* As faith becomes genuinely convinced of God's faithfulness, it does, in fact, affect one's emotional responses, for true faith instigates positive feelings. Paul said in Romans 5:1, "Therefore, since we have been justified through faith, we have peace . . ." He prays in Romans 15:13, "May the God of hope fill you with all joy and peace as you trust in him." *That is knowledge through sensibilities*—though faith, of course, is involved. When God sends His Holy Spirit to the trusting, believing heart and transforms that person, He bears inner witness to the presence of Jesus Christ. By such testimony, He makes the recipient very much aware of that presence. *That is knowledge by awareness.*

Yes, we may know Christ! We may know Him through reading His Word, trusting His promises, and concluding that God is faithful to His promises. We may know Him by sensing His presence, by feeling Him in our hearts (though surely our knowledge of Christ dare not depend upon such feelings alone! It must go deeper than that). And we may know Him by being made aware of His presence by the indwelling Spirit. Paul says in our text, "I want to know Christ . . ." And so do I! Even so—amen!

*PRAYER: Dear Father in heaven, thank you for the privilege of knowing Your Son Jesus. Grant us an ever deepening knowledge of Him. Help us to know Him better and better. We ask this in Jesus' name. Amen.*

WEEK 8: *Thursday*
READ: *Philippians 3:10 again*

## THREE MARKS OF KNOWING CHRIST

In our text, Paul lists three clear marks of knowing Christ. *First, it involves a personal experiencing of the power of His resurrection.* He says, "I want to know Christ and the power of

His resurrection." Any direct, present tense awareness of the presence of Christ which one encounters can only be experienced in direct association with the power of His resurrection. It goes without saying that a dead Christ could make himself known to no one. And so to "know Christ" certainly involves a present and continuous, vibrant faith in the historical fact that Jesus Christ arose bodily from the grave! The preaching of the apostles recorded in the Acts of the Apostles abounds with the promulgation of the good news that the Jesus, who was dead, is now alive—this was the very heart and drive of their proclamation!

But to know Christ in the power of His resurrection implicates more than believing that Christ is living. Faith in the fact that He is alive again also releases that very resurrection power in our hearts even now. In Ephesians 1:19-20, Paul says that we may know "his incomparably great power for us *who believe.* That power is like the working of His mighty strength, which he exerted in Christ when He raised Him from the dead . . ." In other words, the type of power that God wielded when He raised Christ from the dead is the very same which He effects in our hearts even now *if we believe!*

What precisely happens when we believe? God, by His Spirit, breathes into us new resurrection life! Here is the core of the new birth! And all who are now made alive in Christ by faith also live in the hope of the future resurrection, when our bodies will be raised by that same power! How blessed to know Him and the power of His resurrection!

*The second mark of knowing Christ involves a personal willingness to share in His suffering.* He says, "I want to know Christ . . . and the fellowship of sharing in His sufferings . . ." How many of us can assert honestly that we have been called upon to really suffer for Jesus' sake? While in Nigeria I heard a missionary from the country of Chad relate the following incident. In one of the villages of that country lived one Christian among a solidly Moslem populace. Illness struck his child, and it soon became evident that he would have to be hospitalized in a larger nearby city. Only one man in the town owned an automobile. The Christian went to the owner, requesting that he take him and his boy to the hospital. "My car isn't working," was the reply. The Christian offered to pay the entire cost of the trip, but the Moslem insisted again that his car was not in running order. That evening the baby died. As darkness crept upon the village the Christian and the town judge buried the dead child—while the owner of the automobile drove out of the village to the very city where the hospital was located. The only reason he refused to take his neighbor to the city was the fact that he was a Christian. I maintain that that is something of "the fellowship of sharing in His sufferings."

*The third mark of knowing Christ involves a personal conforming to His death.* He says, "I want to know Christ . . . becoming like Him in His death." As Paul expresses his own desire here, can you hear him calling for us who know Him to also be identified with Christ on the cross? He is not insinuating that we must literally die on a wooden cross. But He is prodding us to participate in the spirit of His crucifixion and cross bearing.

Being crucified with Christ concerns us with an inner dying to selfishness, a renouncing of stubbornness against the will of God, completely reversing our unwillingness to fully yield to Christ. It says, "No," to anything that would hinder the will of God from being fulfilled in our lives. The song writer of a former day corners the very issue:

> "Lord, let me die to selfish desires,
> Kindle in me the Pentecost fires;
> Emptied of self and sin may I be,
> Filled with Thy love and hidden in Thee.
> Emptied of self, with holy love filled,
> Let ev'ry voice within me be stilled,
> Until I hear Thy whispers to me,
> Dead to the world but living in Thee."[1]

---

[1]"Emptied of Self" by Haldor Lillenas. Copyright 1919. Ren. 1947 by Lillenas Publishing Company. Used by permission.

This inner crucifixion may vary as to degrees in the lives of different individuals, or at varying states in the Christian's life. But the goal is to be completely yielded and fully crucified! Such a crucifixion involves a wrapping up of everything that is contrary to God's will for us and, from this time forth, reckoning ourselves to be dead to it all for Jesus' sake. This is the implication of "becoming like Him in His death." God grant us all such a spirit!

*PRAYER: Dear Father in heaven, grant us the attitude of crucifixion today. Bestow upon us the grace to carry the cross of Christ and to be totally yielded to Him. We pray that this spirit will mark our lives both now and forever. Amen.*

---

*WEEK 8: Friday*
*READ: Philippians 3:10 once again*

## THREE MEASURES OF KNOWING CHRIST

Let's call to mind again what we have discovered in this verse thus far concerning the privilege of knowing Christ. On Wednesday we gave some thought to THREE METHODS OF KNOWING CHRIST. Yesterday we considered THREE MARKS OF KNOWING CHRIST.

Today we will see how Paul clarifies for us THREE MEASURES OF KNOWING CHRIST. One has to do with *desire*, one with *progress* and one with *culmination.*

*Take the measure of desire first*—this concept of "knowing Christ" was so important to Paul that he was willing to "consider everything a loss compared to the surpassing greatness" of realizing such a relationship. We saw this in verse 8. His willingness to sacrifice anything and all if he could just "know Him" is obvious. And maybe here is the reason that so many people—even religious people—never come to really experience Christ in a deep and meaningful way. It simply and bluntly is just not that important to them yet! Other things have climbed to higher positions on their list of priorities. Christian, sometime we must come to understand clearly that by the very nature of who Christ is and who we are, we must accord Him first place in our lives or He will maintain no place at all for long! Our longing for Him must outweigh our desire for anything or anyone else!

*The measure of progress is next*—the idea expressed in our text by the words, "I want to know Christ," is basically this: "I want in an increasing way to know Christ better and better . . " None of us dare claim that we know Christ as well or as intimately as we might. Nor do we know Him as we will if we continue to follow Him faithfully. A mother holds her baby daughter in her arms. That baby will look up into her mother's face and smile and coo. She learns to recognize that face. And in her little mind she knows her mother. But she does not know her mother nearly as well as she will as the years slip by. She will learn to know her better and better. So it is with knowing Christ.

*Finally the measure of culmination*—Paul says in our text, "I want to know Christ and the power of His resurrection and the fellowship of sharing in His sufferings, becoming like Him in His death, *and so, somehow, to attain to the resurrection from the dead."* Here is the final goal! Here is the culmination of all for which Paul was striving, as expressed in our text. His desire was to have a glorified body, a glorified mind—to be perfect! And then, in his glorified body, he will be able to anticipate coming to know Christ better and better throughout all eternity! The hymn writer burst forth with his assessment of such a hope: "When we've been there ten thousand years, bright shining as the sun; we've no less days to sing God's praise than when we'd first begun!"[1] Oh yes! Can we grasp that truth?

The question we are duty bound to press upon ourselves periodically—and very sincerely—is this: "Am I coming to know Christ in an ever deepening and increasing way?" Again, "Do I know Christ better now than I did last year at this time?" May the Lord in heaven give us His help to know how to be ever growing in the knowledge of our Lord and our Savior, Jesus Christ!

*PRAYER: Lord, to know You is the basic issue of life! Thank you for the privilege of being able to come to experience You in our hearts in this life. We want to know You better. Grant us a deeper desire to be progressing in our knowledge of You that we may look forward to attaining to the resurrection from the dead! We ask this all for Jesus' sake. Amen.*

---

[1] 'Amazing Grace' by John Newton.

```
┌─────────────────────────────────────────────────────────┐
│                                                           │
│     PRESSING ON TOWARD THE GOAL (3:10-16)                 │
│                                                           │
│     Acknowledging Personal Imperfections (3:12)           │
│     Action for Personal Improvement (3:12-14)             │
│     Attitude Toward Personal Illumination (3:15-16)       │
│                                                           │
└─────────────────────────────────────────────────────────┘
```

*WEEK 8: Saturday*
*READ: Philippians 3:10-16*

## PRESSING ON TOWARD THE GOAL

The little boy proudly announced to his father, "Daddy, I don't have to say my prayers any more—I already learned them!" We chuckle. But how often is that oversimplified philosophy fondly cuddled by Christians all the way into adulthood! It gives one such a "comforting sense of accomplishment and security" (though both be counterfeit) to imagine "arrival" in his quest for spiritual maturity. But the dangers accompanying such a mentality are self-evident. The Scriptures remind us often that we will never attain to the level of sainthood in this life from whence we need not be further concerned about additional progress in grace. Today's text is one such reference.

Verses 10 through 16 follow immediately the section where Paul speaks of "knowing Christ." In this division he witnessed to what the experiential knowledge of Jesus Christ meant to him personally. It had generated in him a strong hope to attain to the resurrection of the dead.

Now if such assurance had been designed to liberate us from any further regard about "going on" in one's faith, then Paul, of all people, ought to have been so qualified. But, on the very heels of that section on such assurance, Paul calls for the most energetic type of self-discipline found in the Bible in order to "keep on progressing in Christ." And his eye is fixed on that final goal of attaining "to the resurrection from the dead"!

What we Christians may be prone to forget at times is that, though our salvation is all of grace, nevertheless, in order to *grow* in that relationship with Christ, we must agree to fully cooperate with God—cooperation is the issue! A man entered a gun shop. He was planning to go bear hunting and wanted to be free from any doubt that the gun he purchased could, for certain, kill a bear. Holding up a special model designed for bears and large game, the man asked, "Are you sure if I carry this gun with me I will not be eaten by a bear?" "No question about it, young man," the gun salesman replied dryly,"—if you carry it fast enough!" You see, cooperation is the issue, sir! Cooperation is the issue!

In our text, Paul speaks of such agreement with God. For the next three days we want to consider this whole subject of cooperating with the heavenly Father in order to successfully press on toward our final goal. Tomorrow we will see the importance of ACKNOWLEDGING PERSONAL IMPERFECTIONS. On Monday we will work through the importance of ACTION FOR PERSONAL IMPROVEMENT. And finally, on Tuesday we will examine the importance of our ATTITUDE TOWARD PERSONAL ILLUMINATION. Let us be praying that God will give us special understanding as we grapple with the thought of how to effectively press on toward the goal!

*PRAYER: Our Father in heaven, we understand Your Word to teach us that there is no place to cease in our striving to continually walk with You. We thank You for daily grace. We thank You for inner strength to persevere. Give us help today to press on toward our goal with our eyes fixed on Jesus Christ, in whose name we pray. Amen.*

## ACKNOWLEDGING PERSONAL IMPERFECTIONS

If we expect to effectively "press toward the goal," it first of all must involve a necessary ACKNOWLEDGEMENT OF PERSONAL IMPERFECTIONS. Read carefully verse 12: "Not that I have already obtained all this, or have already been made perfect . . ." Look at verse 13 also: "Brothers, I do not consider myself yet to have taken hold of it . . ." Here is an open acknowledgement on the part of Paul, that he was not yet as perfect as he expected to be some day! We catch the feeling that he was fully expecting to be "more perfect" some day than he was at the time of penning these lines.

If we are to grasp an understanding of this statement in the light of its complete context, we must, of necessity, reread verse 10 with verse 11: "I want to know Christ and the power of His resurrection and the fellowship of sharing in His sufferings, becoming like Him in His death, and so, somehow, to attain to the resurrection from the dead . . ." Then he proceeds with today's text: "Not that I have already obtained all this, or have already been made perfect . . ." Let us paraphrase his thought: "Not that I know Christ like I want to, or have shared His sufferings as I might or have become like Him in His death as I should, or certainly not that I have been resurrected!"

If the Apostle Paul was willing to be so transparent as to offer such a confession, it seems quite likely that for us to recognize and confess the same could not help but lay a proper foundation for spiritual good in our lives. Notwithstanding our full consecration and obedience to God, our faith and sincere efforts to please the one we love supremely, *we are not what we could be and ought to be!* It is said that Tennyson spent 17 years writing "in memorium" and that some parts he wrote and re-wrote as often as 100 times. And then, when he released it to the publisher, he was dismayed by a feeling of dissatisfaction.[1] Such a spirit marks one of the secrets of true greatness! The person who is convinced that he has "already been made perfect," and has "already (fully) obtained all this" of which Paul speaks in our text, is the one who will least recognize his need for any further spiritual improvement—and he desperately needs it more than anyone else!

Now for a perturbing question: "Is there a contradiction, then, between what Paul confesses in verse 12 and what he states in verse 15?" In verse 15 Paul asserts, "All of us who are mature (KJ, 'perfect') should take such a view of things." The word in verse 12 translated "perfect" and this one in verse 15 rendered "mature" or "perfect" (KJ) are both the same root word. And the meaning is quite evident, of course. It means "to become perfect" or "mature." In verse 12 he has stated that he is not perfect or completely mature. In verse 15, then, he includes himself and says, "All of us who are mature or perfect should take such a view of things." Does this sound contradictory to you?

Not at all! At least five different types of maturity and perfection are spoken of in the Scriptures—the type and degree in each reference depends upon its usage in the context:

1. The Scriptures refer to *absolute perfection.* This is perfection and maturity to the infinite. Only God possesses such completeness and excellence.

2. They speak of *angelic perfection.* Only angels possess this type. Christians will never be angels, not in this world, nor in the world to come.

3. Again, they allude to *Adamic perfection.* This is the perfection and maturity Adam possessed before the fall. We lost this when our first parents fell, and have never regained it.

4. There is *resurrection perfection.* Here is the kind of maturity and perfection we will possess at the resurrection when we will be given glorified bodies.

---

[1]From *Devotional Studies in Philippians* by Lehman Strauss. Copyright © 1976 by Loizeaux Brothers, p. 179. Used by permission.

5. Finally, the Bible calls for *Christian perfection.* Christian perfection is a relative type which one may attain in the process of continually being perfected and maturing. It has to do with one's love for God and his relationship with Him. It involves being born of the Spirit, filled with the Spirit and growing in the Spirit!

So it is not contradictory at all for Paul to speak of those who are mature (perfect), including himself, and at the same time acknowledge that he is not yet perfect (mature). Neither is it contradictory for one who is fully yielded to God and full of the Holy Spirit, who loves God with all his heart, at the same time to be unable to always produce perfect actions or exercise mature judgment. The perfection and maturity which he possesses relates only to his love for God, not to his ability to perfectly demonstrate that love outwardly.

On the other hand, let us not misunderstand Paul at this point! His acknowledgement of imperfection does not offer us a stamped license to contentedly live our whole lives pampering such shortcomings! This whole section is full of Paul's deep purpose "to keep on going on" to continual improvement! This must include sincere effort, by God's grace, to conquer such deficiencies! By the grace of God let us be doing the same!

*PRAYER: Dear Father in heaven, we know that we have not yet attained. We know that we are not yet perfect. Grant us grace to be striving. Give us help to be growing. Make this a day of definite improvement in some area of our lives. And may that progress be one more step in coming to maturity! We ask this in Jesus Christ's name. Amen.*

## ACTION FOR PERSONAL IMPROVEMENT

Yesterday we considered the necessity of ACKNOWL-EDGING PERSONAL IMPERFECTIONS if we expect to be intent upon effectively pressing toward our final goal. Today we will note the importance of ACTION FOR PERSONAL IMPROVEMENT.

Many of us Christians are like the man who spent his life thinking and planning for his "dream vacation." When asked when he and his wife would actually be leaving, his reply was always, "As soon as I get plans completed." No one was surprised when the man died, never having taken his "holiday leave." He was too busy thinking and planning to take any time for action.

Look at verse 12. Paul says, "Not that I have already obtained all this, or have already been made perfect, *but I press on . . .*" Read verses 13 and 14: "Brothers, I do not consider myself yet to have taken hold of it. But one thing I do . . . I press on toward the goal . . ."

The idea of the word used in verse 12 and verse 13, translated "I press on," is that of "pursuing," as a runner who sets his eye on the finish line and hurls himself straight toward that mark. It is "to drive oneself out of deep passionate devotion." So what is Paul urging upon himself? I believe we can paraphrase his thought this way: "I acknowledge that I have not yet obtained all that is involved in knowing Christ as I want to. I have certainly not taken hold of the resurrection yet either—but, out of deep passionate devotion to Christ, I drive myself on toward that goal!" And we cannot read his statement without catching the suggestion that we, too, ought to be so motivated.

Put your eye on verse 12 again: ". . . but I press on to take hold of that for which Christ Jesus took hold of me." Christ has "laid hold" of you and me, too, that we might someday share in a mighty resurrection! But we are not there yet. So we must "press on"! Who is he who dreams, "If I can just be truly converted and genuinely filled with the Holy Spirit I will then have all I need—I will have arrived—the battle will be over"? Oh no! The battle will then have just begun! You and I are not able to avow that we know Him as well as we ought to know Him yet. And we certainly cannot say we have already been resurrected. So let us fix our eyes on the goal and press on and on!

The question then is this: "Exactly what becomes necessary if we are to successfully press on toward the goal?" Paul informs us that we must develop a two-fold attitude—one which takes a particular view toward the past, and another which looks positively toward the future.

*Concerning our attitude toward the past*, Paul says that, while we are pressing on toward the goal, we must "forget what is behind." If we are to keep aggressively "moving ahead" spiritually, some things we simply must forget! We must forget our past sins and failures which God has forgiven. Satan smirks with glee when he is able to succeed in continually haunting a Christian over some failure of the past (though God has completely forgiven). If he can cut short that child of God from "forgiving himself," he rests assured that he will continue to punish himself "for suffering such a defeat." And he also knows that such a morbid attitude over the past will short circuit any effectiveness the Christian may hope to exert in his witness for Christ.

Of all men, Paul must have faced such temptation. Before his conversion he had committed the most disgraceful of sins. Had he chosen to brood over them, his attitude would have driven him to despair. He had innocent blood on his hands. But God through mercy had forgiven him! And he chose to forgive himself!

For some, possibly, the most difficult to forget of the incidents of the past are not the failures, but the successes! If we want to keep "going on" we cannot afford to live on the laurels of the past. We must discipline ourselves to live in the victory of the present.

*What then ought our attitude be toward the future?* Catch the implication of Paul's words: "Straining toward what is ahead . . ." It can be translated, "Stretching forward . . ." The hymn writer expresses the same thought: "Awake, my soul, stretch every nerve, and press with vigor on."[1] Here is certainly not the picture of one who is apprehensive about what the future may hold—or afraid of what God might ask of him if he follows His Son carefully and sincerely. This idea of "straining toward what is ahead" depicts one who is anxious to receive all that God has for him and to be all that He wants him to be! It portrays the concept of abandoning oneself to the one who holds the future!

What all is involved in such a forward looking attitude? Well, it would intimate a careful searching of God's Word for His guidance in one's life. It must certainly include the sincere seeking of God's will in prayer. It should anticipate willing obedience to new light. It would demand of us an ever-enlarging faith. It must push us to more effective and faithful witnessing. It would include sincere effort on our part to climb on top of feelings of inferiority or inability. It must involve "pressing on and on"!

In a small church yard at the foot of one of the great mountains of Switzerland, lies buried the body of a young Englishman who was killed while making an ascent. On the tombstone, under his name and dates of birth and death, the following inscription is carved: "He died climbing."[2] That is the thought! Someday Jesus will come or death will overtake us—let's be sure that, in either case, He will find us climbing!

So we have seen the necessary ACTION FOR PERSONAL IMPROVEMENT! May God give us His help and drive us to such performance!

*PRAYER: Dear Father in heaven, through the power of Your*

---

[1] "Awake My Soul, Stretch Every Nerve" by Philip Dodridge.

[2] From *Devotional Studies in Philippians* by Lehman Strauss. Copyright © 1976 by Loizeaux Brothers, p. 189. Used by permission.

*Holy Spirit, breathe into us a divine drive, an incentive, a will to press on! Give us much grace. Never let us be satisfied with our present attainment in such grace. Help us to take action for personal improvement. We want, today, to continue to stretch every nerve to press on toward our final goal. Amen.*

---

*WEEK 9: Tuesday*
*READ: Philippians 3:10-16 (consider verses 15-16)*

## ATTITUDE TOWARD PERSONAL ILLUMINATION

We have found that attaining the final goal will not come about automatically for the Christian. For the past two days we have given thought to the necessity of ACKNOWLEDGING PERSONAL IMPERFECTIONS, as well as taking ACTION FOR PERSONAL IMPROVEMENT, if we intend to effectively press on toward our ultimate objective. Today we will give attention to a proper ATTITUDE TOWARD PERSONAL ILLUMINATION, so essential also for such spiritual progress. In verses 15 and 16 we read, "All of us who are mature should take such a view of things. And if on some point you think differently, that too God will make clear to you. Only let us live up to what we have already attained."

Get the thought—"If on some point you think differently, that too God will make clear to you." Here is divine illumination.

Note carefully—we do not hear Paul demanding of Christians here that they continually be testing themselves, "looking within" in order to ascertain whether they are able to "pass certain religious examinations." He is not even suggesting that they be constantly "taking their spiritual temperatures." None of that!

It seems to me that some Christians imbibe a certain subtle delight (morbid satisfaction) in participating in a chronic attempt to "find something wrong" in their relationship with Christ. Paul is simply and positively urging us, in this total context, to count everything but loss for Christ. Forget the past. Stretch forward toward the future and press on toward the goal! And if on some point we think differently than we ought, God will take it on himself to make that clear to us. The burden of such correction rests with Him!

What then should be our attitude if, as we are following on, God, in fact, does reveal to our hearts that there is some point on which we are "thinking differently (are otherwise minded)"? We might not have been aware previously of such error in our thinking (which has probably affected our practice). But now God reveals this fact to the inner soul and spirit. And He says, "At this point, you are missing the mark." Now, at that juncture, God's revelation has become new light. We now become accountable to "walk in that light" by simple obedience. It may be some practice or habit, or it may involve some deep attitude. It could constitute some association or something concerning God's will for our future. Here is divine illumination!

Such a revelation of new light from God does not insinuate that the recipient is not a Spirit-filled Christian. God is simply clarifying to him that an area in his life exists about which he is "thinking differently" than God thinks. What response does God expect? He anticipates that His child will keep on "moving ahead, walking in the light" (1 John 1:7). He will insist that he not endeavor to side-step such an issue, but rather face such new illumination, welcome it and walk on in obedience!

A new pastor assumed his duties with his happy, expectant congregation, welcomed by a large vote. He preached his first sermon, and people smiled and nodded and shook his hand. The next Sunday a segment of the people were taken back somewhat when he preached the same sermon—and they became quite skeptical when, on the third Sunday, they heard it again! Upon the fourth reception of the identical message a delegation decided it was now time to speak to the board of deacons. One of the leaders, appointed by the rest, dutifully spoke to the new pastor. "Pastor," he said, "we realize you have been busy with moving and unpacking. However, we think that it is now time you preach a different sermon than the one you have given us for four Sundays. Do you not feel you should consider this request?" The pastor looked the deacon in the eye as he responded, "When you begin to walk in the light of the first sermon I have given, I will then give a new one. Until then, a new sermon will do you no good!" This was rash action! Indeed, I do not know how long that pastor remained at his new charge. But his point was well taken!

God is not obligated to lavish us with more light until we are willing to obey all that He has already flashed across our pathway! One of the greatest problems of the church is perceived in the fact that so many of God's people are so politely "walking behind so much light." May God help us to respond positively to His divine illumination to our hearts. Let us constantly pull on His grace that we may be enabled to "walk in the light as He is in the light," that we may continually have fellowship with Him and each other, and enjoy perpetual cleansing from sin by the blood of Christ!

PRAYER: Dear Father in heaven, illuminate our hearts and our minds with the light of Your Word. Give us grace to obey that light. And may the Holy Spirit's presence continually empower us to take a proper attitude toward such personal enlightenment. Thank you for Your presence this day, in Jesus' name. Amen.

EXAMPLES OF ANOTHER WORLD (3:17-21)

Imitation of Christ's Company (3:17)
Recognition of Christ's Enemy (3:18-19)
Identification with Christ's Community (3:20)
Anticipation Through Christ's Victory (3:20b-21)

WEEK 9: Wednesday
READ: Philippians 3:17-21

## EXAMPLES OF ANOTHER WORLD

The answer to a hypothetical question that we might pose to ourselves at the outset of our study of this particular segment might be enlightening: "What if, by some quirk of fate, all of a sudden, everyone in the congregation of which we are members would become just like us? What sort of church would result?" Not many of us would be totally convinced that that type of switch would enhance the image of our company of believers sufficiently enough to make it worth it all. Few of us would be tempted to feel that we have always been the prime A-1 examples of what the personality, attitude and conduct of a Christian ought to be—especially under some of the circumstances we found ourselves this past month.

We just concluded a section last week in which Paul himself openly and humbly confessed that he had not attained the measure of maturity and perfection he wanted to either—*but he was pressing on* toward the mark for the prize for which God had called him!

Maybe, on the other hand, we would demonstrate a bit more objectivity if we could rephrase the question: "How would you like to reproduce what has happened to you and your faith in the lives of everyone in your church?" Would you hope that everyone in your congregation could discover what you have found in Christ? My own conviction is that, unless we deeply want what has happened to us in our relationships with the Savior to happen to everyone, probably too little has happened to us! If we do not genuinely believe in what has taken place in us, nobody will! One fact is crystal clear—while Paul did not feel that he had already attained that measure of maturity and perfection that he wanted, he certainly did, nevertheless, completely believe in what had happened in his heart and life through Christ! And he believed that what had transpired in his heart ought to happen to everyone!

This fact shines through clearly in his opening statement of today's text. "Join with others in following my example," he urges with confidence. Then he proceeds with four further ideas which are related to this first statement. We want to give some attention to those thoughts over the next four days. Tomorrow we will see how he calls for the IMITATION OF CHRIST'S COMPANY. Our need for a RECOGNITION OF CHRIST'S ENEMY will take our attention on Friday. Then on Saturday and Sunday we will examine his call for our IDENTIFICATION WITH CHRIST'S COMMUNITY and our ANTICIPATION THROUGH CHRIST'S VICTORY. Again let us be asking for the guidance of the Holy Spirit as we, together, apply ourselves to understanding this section of God's Word.

*PRAYER: Gracious Lord Jesus Christ, Son of the living God, we know that our greatest task in this life is to properly represent You to a world that does not know You. You want us to be examples of another world—the heavenly. And to be that type of sample, we need the indwelling Spirit and the grace that comes from above. Fill us with Your grace, fill us with Your Spirit. Help us to represent You well today. We ask this in Jesus' name. Amen.*

*WEEK 9: Thursday*
*READ: Philippians 3:17-21 (give attention to verse 17)*

## IMITATION OF CHRIST'S COMPANY

"Hold your bat like this!" ordered the ten-year-old would-be home-run king to his buddy. "But I don't want to hold it that way," Johnny retorted, "I want to hold it this way!" "But that's not the way George Brett does it!" shot back the first with as much authority and cocksureness as he could muster. "I don't care," was Johnny's defensive response, "I don't want to be a copycat!" And there is a streak of Johnny's spirit in all of us, isn't there? Most of us would hope to become more in life than a set of ditto marks!

Paul has been misinterpreted in today's text to mean precisely such mimicry when he calls the Christians at Philippi, and those of all ages, to the IMITATION OF CHRIST'S COMPANY. Read verse 17 again: "Join with others in following my example, brothers, and take note of those who live according to the pattern we gave you." The very literal translation of that first phrase might be, "Be fellow imitators of me," or "Be my fellow imitators."

Now does that smack of audacity to you? Does Paul turn you off? Does he sound egotistical? If he means, "Look at me, I am your best specimen of Christianity around—just copycat me!"— then we might have valid cause to question his motives and suspicion his pride. I reject such an interpretation of his words here. I personally believe he displays the same thought in this verse that he did in Acts 26:29 when Agrippa asked him, "Do you think that in such a short time you can persuade me to be a Christian?" And Paul responded, "Short time or long—I pray God that not only you but all who are listening to me today may become what I am, except for these chains." What is he saying? Is he insinuating that, since his example is flawless, these who heard him should just begin to parrot the way he performed? I don't believe so at all! He is saying, "I have become a true Christian, Agrippa, and I wish you would too—I wish you would become what I am, and I wish all who are listening to me would do the same. I wish you would *all* become Christians!"

So here in today's text we have the same motive. He had stated in the previous context, "I have not obtained all this and am not perfect, but I press on—I forget the things behind and, straining toward what is ahead, I press on toward the goal." Now he says, "Imitate my example in this! You, too, keep pressing on toward the goal. Follow my example. Forget the past, reach ahead, keep on going!"

Good example breeds tremendous power! Tertullian, one of the great church fathers, said that he, and most of the converts who came out of paganism in his day, were won to Christ, not by books or sermons, but by observing how Christians lived and died.[1] Paul challenges us in our text, "Follow my example, brothers, and take note of those who live according to the pattern we gave you." Take note! Mark them!

Certain people have stamped a lasting, positive influence for good on my life. I have "taken note" of these. Their attitudes were positive and forward looking. They were able to forget the past failures and look forward to the future in confidence. They possessed buoyant faith and their goals were to simply glorify Jesus Christ and to attain to the resurrection from the dead. Without fail, they have carved out a lasting impression on my life that has been good and positive. I praise them! I have "taken note" of the other type also. They have, in almost every case, dented my life with an influence that has been negative. In both cases, there have been those with whom I agreed theologically and those with whom I disagreed. To me, theology has always been quite important. It matters to me what one believes about God. But when I recall those who have influenced my life, I must personally confess that it has not been so much

---

[1] From *A Treasury of Sermon Illustrations* edited by Charles L. Wallis. Copyright renewal © 1978 by Charles L. Wallis, p. 111. Used by permission of the publishers, Abingdon Press.

what they taught me with their lips about God that has influenced me the *most*. It has been what they taught me with their lives that has left the abiding impression!

In our text Paul is calling, first of all, for our IMITATION OF CHRIST'S COMPANY! *"Take note* of those who live according to the pattern we gave you." Let *those* be the ones who influence your life for good!

*PRAYER: Dear Father in heaven, we know that our lives are influencing others. We are either influencing them for good in a positive way, or for evil in a negative way, making it more difficult for them to be Christians. Fill us with the Holy Spirit that the influence of our lives today will make it easy for others to want to be Christians. We ask this in Jesus' name. Amen.*

———————————————•◆•———————————————

*WEEK 9: Friday*
*READ: Philippians 3:17-21 (note verses 18 and 19)*

### RECOGNITION OF CHRIST'S ENEMY

Yesterday we saw the need for our IMITATION OF CHRIST'S COMPANY. Today we shall reckon with our need of RECOGNIZING CHRIST'S ENEMY. Paul says in verse 18, "For, as I have told you before and now say again even with tears, many live as enemies of the cross of Christ . . ." And he proceeds in verse 19 to describe their destiny, their gods, their glory and their thinking. Again, at this point in his letter, Paul spits out some very strong statements of an extremely caustic nature. But note quickly that he is making these remarks "even with tears." It has been said that we ought to periodically hear preaching on hell and judgment—but never without tears! True! At least never without compassion!

Now for a background to Paul's comments in these verses. Previously in this letter Paul has countered the false teachings of _legalism_ and has warned against the results of such in one's life. Here he tackles the problem of _license_! The first involved the misapplication of law—the second, the abuse of liberty!

The Gnostics were, in all probability, the objects of his pen in this section. This body of religionists believed that all material was evil and that all spirit was good. Since the body was material, it was evil. Though one be a genuine Christian, they taught, he lived in an evil body.

Two thought patterns were predominant among the Gnostics, springing from this "spirit" and "body" concept: one held that when Christ saved, He saved the spirit. They reasoned that one might just as well give vent to his passions in sinful living, for it was the spirit that really counted. The only way to be rid of sin was to be rid of the body! The other school abused grace. They asserted that though one go on in his life of flagrant sinning, no matter! Why? For the more he sinned the more God's grace must come into play to forgive—thus, the more he sinned, the more God's grace must abound in forgiveness. So "let's keep on sinning that grace may abound more and more"!

Now remember, back in verses 2 through 9, Paul was very blunt in his rejection of legalism. The legalists claimed that one must be saved by his works. Paul called them "dogs" and went on to declare that we must consider all of our good works as loss and be made righteous before God by faith alone! But here he is just as blunt in his rejection of the opposite extreme. To assert that, since one is saved by faith, his good works do not really matter at all misses the mark by every bit the margin as did legalism. To maintain that it really doesn't matter how one lives so long as he "just keeps believing" will reap devastating results! "But I want to *guard* against legalism," one may boast. Then do not fear, for what you propagate is certainly not legalism! It is libertarianism!

To interpret Paul to teach that if one places his faith in Christ, it really will not make any difference as to his life style is to completely abuse his teaching of salvation by grace through faith! It will make all the difference in his eternity! And Paul is warning of this very fact.

Listen to how he describes those who teach such liberalism—and remember, he does so with tears! He calls them "enemies of the cross of Christ." Though they profess to be "for Him" they are "against Him." They pose as "friends" of the gospel. They practice as its "foes." "Their destiny is destruction!" This expresses that which is completely opposite to eternal safety. It is eternal loss—not eternal loss of being, but eternal loss of well-being. "Their god is their stomach"—an expression used to describe sensual or fleshly appetites, the pampering of all physical drives. "Their glory is in their shame." They do not recognize that that which has actually brought shame and disgrace upon them is the very thing in which they glory. "Their mind is on earthly things." They are geared entirely to this earth and "earthiness" as opposed to "heavenly realities." What a description!

Paul is leveling his charge against those who misuse and abuse God's good grace! In this context, he is pleading for us to recognize all such as Christ's enemies. It is a fearful warning. His words are not lifting, but they are profitable to the soul. Let us read and benefit thereby.

*PRAYER: Dear Father in heaven, help us to receive this warning willingly. Help us to be careful that we may recognize those who would lead us astray. Grant us wisdom and the knowledge of the unadulterated Word of God that we may overcome error with the truth. Make this principle very practical to us in our lives, in Jesus' name we pray. Amen.*

*WEEK 9: Saturday*
*READ: Philippians 3:17-21 again (look at verse 20)*

## IDENTIFICATION WITH CHRIST'S COMMUNITY

For the past two days we have been studying how, as examples of another world, we must IMITATE CHRIST'S COMPANY and RECOGNIZE CHRIST'S ENEMY. Today we will see the necessity of our IDENTIFICATION WITH CHRIST'S COMMUNITY. Read again Paul's statement in verse 20: "But our citizenship is in heaven . . ." Literally that phrase may be rendered, "Our place of citizenship is in the heavenlies . . ."

I know the feeling of being a very real part of a country of which I was not a citizen. My wife and I were missionaries in the wonderful country of Nigeria for four years. We learned to love the people deeply and to sincerely appreciate that country—but it was not home.

Throughout the Roman empire of Paul's day lived certain special people who, either by birth or by special recognition, were citizens of the capital city. They resided in many cities throughout the empire—but they shared one honor, their citizenship was in Rome. And wherever they lived, they were expected to conduct themselves in such a way that would bring respect both to the city of Rome and to the emperor. Paul himself, though a blood Jew, was a Roman citizen. We read this in Acts 16:37-38 and 22:25-28. And it is to this analogy that he appeals when he says that, while we are on earth, in a foreign country, "our citizenship is in heaven."

I read an article in the newspaper sometime ago that touched me deeply. The opening lines read, "Daniel Kelly, home for the first day of his 38 years of life, is dazzled. 'I never thought it would be like this,' China-born Kelly said Tuesday night when he stepped from a plane." The article went on to state that Kelly had spent 21 of his 38 years in mainland China labor camps. His crimes—refusal to renounce his U.S. citizenship and an escape attempt.

*JOY IN A ROMAN JAIL*

Kelly had been born in China, the son of an American missionary and a Chinese mother. His only knowledge of the United States had been through books. His father had died in 1957. He tried to escape from China once but was caught and sentenced to a labor camp. His sister wrote to him from the United States continually, though for six years the letters did not get through. He answered, but for long periods of time the letters did not come out of China. Through it all he refused Chinese citizenship, maintaining his identification with the United States. When the ordeal was over and he had arrived in his homeland, he declared, "It was worth it!"[1]

Paul's statement in our text parallels this article. When we were born again our heavenly Father, the eternal citizen of heaven, issued us birthrights to a heavenly citizenship. We were then heaven-born and are now heaven-bound. Though we have never seen the city of our allegiance, our Father expects us to be completely loyal, both in conduct and attitude, to the land of our birthright. Under no circumstances are we to renounce that citizenship in order to accept any recognition foreign to that of our heavenly homeland. One fact is certain— the airwaves of communication with the community of our citizenship are open even now. We may contact heaven daily. And someday a blessed home-going will transpire. When we get to heaven, the place of our citizenship, our response will betray much more elation than did Daniel Kelly when he landed in the United States! We, too, shall exclaim, "I never thought it would be like this! It was worth it all!"

Let us keep our identification with Christ's community intact. Let us ever be looking up remembering that we belong to another world. "Our citizenship is in heaven!" Bless His holy name!

*PRAYER: Lord Jesus Christ, we thank You for the privilege of being identified with Your city, and Your cause. Remind us often of our heavenly citizenship. Help us to live today*

---

[1]Indianapolis (UPI) story entitled, "Kelly Comes Home to a Strange Land," January, 1978; taken from *The Elkhart Truth*, published in Elkhart, Indiana.

*as citizens of that other world. Grant us grace to do nothing that would embarrass our heavenly Father or bring a blight upon our homeland. Thank you for the love that makes such a relationship possible, in Jesus' name. Amen.*

**WEEK 10: Sunday**
*READ: Philippians 3:17-21 one more time (consider verses*
*20b and 21)*

### ANTICIPATION THROUGH CHRIST'S VICTORY

In today's text, Paul urges us to a type of wonderful AN-TICIPATION THROUGH CHRIST'S VICTORY! Let us read verses 20b and 21 carefully: "And we eagerly await a Savior from there, the Lord Jesus Christ, who, by the power that enables him to bring everything under his control, will transform our lowly bodies so that they may be like his glorious body!" This has been the goal of this entire section. Every attitude and sacrifice Paul has himself assumed, and required of us, has had as its purpose the reaching of the final goal—that of finally being a part of the resurrection!

And what does Paul say will take place on that day of resurrection? "We eagerly await a Savior from there . . ." So the first incident that will transpire is that Jesus Christ will come back from heaven. The two angels dressed in white declared to the disciples when Jesus returned to heaven, "This same Jesus, who has been taken from you into heaven, will come back in the same way you have seen him go into heaven" (Acts 1:11b). He himself had said, "And if I go and prepare a place for you, I will come back and take you to be with me that you also may be where I am" (John 14:3).

What else will transpire? "By the power that enables him to bring everything under his control, (He) will transform our lowly bodies so that they will be like his glorious body." We will receive glorified bodies—bodies just like the resurrected body of Jesus! What a marvelous hope!

What should our attitude be then when we consider the second coming of Christ? It is distressing that so many Christians, who really come to grips with the possibility that Jesus may actually come back before they expect Him, become frightened and unnerved! Now, friends, that should not be! Paul says we ought to be "eagerly awaiting" His coming—that is anticipation, an attitude which hopes that Jesus will come soon!

Our inner reaction toward the possible soon return of Jesus Christ makes for one dependable gauge of our spiritual temperature. Show me a person who fears His coming, and I will show you a person who needs to examine his soul. Either he senses a type of guilt in his heart (with which he ought to deal) or else he does not understand the second coming of the Lord. Show me a person who can say with John the revelator, "Even so, come quickly, Lord Jesus," and I will show you a person whose heart is warm, and truly right with God.

So we have seen in our study during these past five days true examples of another world are they who imitate those of Christ's company, who recognize Christ's enemy, identify with Christ's community and anticipate Christ's victory! Are we such samples? Are these our attitudes? Are we striving for such a well-rounded outlook in life? Are we concerned about properly representing the world where our citizenship is intact? May God give us His grace and His help to do so with joy!

*PRAYER: Dear Lord Jesus in heaven, we are on earth and we*

*are looking up, anticipating Your return. Help us to eagerly await Your coming and live with such expectation that its joy will be manifest in our lives. Thank you for such a hope, in Jesus' name. Amen.*

---

## GUIDELINES TO GODLINESS (4:1-4)

**Be Faithful in the Lord (4:1)**
**Be Peaceful in the Lord (4:2-3)**
**Be Joyful in the Lord (4:4)**

WEEK 10: Monday
READ: Philippians 4:1-4

## GUIDELINES TO GODLINESS

Let's review. The last half of chapter 3 saw Paul urging all believers to formulate a positive attitude toward the past and the future as we press toward the ultimate goal of final resurrection. His eye has been focused above, primarily on the future. "Forget the past," he says, "and strain for what is ahead." And he assures us, that if in anything our attitude is missing the mark, God will reveal this to us. Then a terse warning concerning the enemies of Christ precedes his final statement that our true citizenship is in the heavenlies! And from there we are waiting for the Savior to come who, by His power, will transform our present bodies so they will be like His glorified body!

We now enter chapter 4. Paul will continue with a number of further exhortations—but now with his eye focused back to earth. These admonitions continue through verse 9, and are geared to helping us become better Christians here and now. They zero in on practical open collar, shirt sleeve Christian living.

For the next three days we will look at the four statements given in these first four verses. They cover three main thoughts —three guidelines to Godliness. Three times the phrase "in the Lord" is used. Once he says, "Stand firm in the Lord." Again he urges, "Agree in the Lord." And a third time he encourages us to "Rejoice in the Lord."

So, basically, what Paul is saying in these verses can be stated this way: "BE FAITHFUL IN THE LORD, BE PEACEFUL IN THE LORD, and BE JOYFUL IN THE LORD." On Tuesday, Wednesday and Thursday we will consider one of these thoughts each day. Each constitutes a guideline to Godliness, so let us purpose to profit by this study so that our lives will, in fact, truly become more "God-like."

*PRAYER: Jesus, our Savior, we thank You for the joy of Your salvation and for the guidance the Word of God gives us for our everyday living. As we study these guidelines to Godliness, breathe upon us by Your Spirit. And rivet to our hearts the principles involved in each of them. We will give You the praise and honor for answering us, in Jesus' name. Amen.*

WEEK 10: *Tuesday*
READ: *Philippians 4:1-4 (read verse 1 again)*

## BE FAITHFUL IN THE LORD

Paul's first exhortation to Godliness in this section is this: BE FAITHFUL IN THE LORD! In verse 1 he pushes us with this statement: "Therefore, my brothers, you whom I love and long for, my joy and crown, that is how you should stand firm in the Lord, dear friends." He is referring back to the all inclusive statement of verses 12 through 21 of the previous chapter—"that is how you should stand firm in the Lord."

Note, first, how Paul's deep feelings of appreciation for these saints at Philippi become apparent in this verse. He claims them as "brothers" and says he "loves" them. He "longs" for them. He affectionately calls them "dear friends." He looks upon them as his "joy and crown." We sense a taste of the same tribute here that we find in another letter Paul penned to the body of believers at Thessalonica, to whom he wrote in I Thessalonians 2:19, "For what is our hope, our joy, or the crown in which we would glory in the presence of our Lord Jesus Christ when he comes? Is it not you? Indeed, you are our glory and joy."

A significant number of these Christians Paul had convinced and brought to Christ himself. He had shared in the spiritual victories and failures of most of them. A bond of fellowship had developed which time and tests had strengthened. Many present-day believers are able to identify with the emotional frame of mind Paul displays here. With absolutely no disrespect for relatives, Christians often confess that the mutual fellowship enjoyed with God's people goes deeper than that which they feel even with their own family members. Why? Because those family members have never given their faith to Christ and their interests are not spiritually inclined.

So these endearing expressions of esteem for the believers at Philippi only add an element of genuineness to his primary consideration at this instance. In today's text Paul's most pressing concern is this: though one may be genuinely regenerated and filled with the Holy Spirit, appreciating the mutual fellowship of partner-believers and growing in the Lord, he is, nonetheless, never beyond the pull of temptation or the danger of cowardice. We are all very much aware that in the presence of some people, and under certain given circumstances, to do what is right comes much easier than in other settings. And we also know that we are acquainted with some persons in whose presence it becomes very difficult to bravely and candidly do what is honest and upright. In this context, Paul is pointing back to what he has said in the previous chapter and he declares, "That is how you should stand firm in the Lord, dear friends."

Did you get the thought? "Stand firm in the Lord!" Faithfulness under extreme pressure—that is the issue Paul is pressing! Barclay points out that the word for *"stand fast* is the word which would be used for a soldier standing fast in the shock of battle, with the enemy surging down upon him!"[1] But where does the real secret of such winning lie? "Stand firm *in the Lord!"* There it is: "in the Lord!" Our only protection against temptation is found in the Lord. It is experienced by always trusting His presence and power! We must abide in Christ and lean upon His grace!

I will never forget hearing the public testimony of a young man shortly after I was converted. I believe he was sincere. But he was sadly misled. His witness went something like this: "I am glad the Lord saved me and I don't care how the devil tempts me, I'm going to be faithful to God! And I'm not going to say that I will be faithful 'by His grace' because I have that determination to follow Him." His sincerity may have been genuine, but the fact remains that he soon faded out of the picture, a victim of the very temptation he did not fear. He found what all discover who are convinced that they can resist

---

[1] From *The Letters to the Philippians, Colossians, and Thessalonians* (Revised Edition), translated and interpreted by William Barclay. Copyright © 1975 William Barclay. Published in the U.S.A. by The Westminster Press, p. 71. Used and adapted by permission.

temptation in their own strength—grit without grace results in gross failure every time!

So Paul is urging us to be faithful. Oh yes, let us be faithful! But let us be faithful *in the Lord!* Let us always recognize that our conquest over temptation can be experienced only as we are "in Him."

*PRAYER: Dear Father in heaven, we thank You that Jesus Christ was faithful to Your plan and Your will. He is our example and our Savior! Grant us grace today to be faithful in Him. Help us to stand firm in the Lord and to be loyal to His cause, out of love. We ask this in Jesus' name. Amen.*

*WEEK 10: Wednesday*
*READ: Philippians 4:1-4 again (focus attention on verses 2 and 3)*

### BE PEACEFUL IN THE LORD

Yesterday our thoughts centered on Paul's admonition that we be FAITHFUL IN THE LORD. Today we will study his second exhortation to Godliness: BE PEACEFUL IN THE LORD. In verse 2 we read, "I plead with Euodia and I plead with Syntyche to agree with each other in the Lord . . ."

It would be enlightening if we knew a little more of the background to what is stated here. We do know from what is expressed in verse 3 that Euodia and Syntyche were two women who had played leading roles in the cause of the gospel at Philippi. Paul says of these ladies in verse 3 that they had "contended at (his) side in the cause of the gospel . . ." They were apparently involved in some type of ministry. Some have suggested that possibly two of the house congregations which existed in Philippi met in their homes.

Does it seem a bit surprising to you to read of two women exercising such a leading influence in the affairs of this early church—especially when most of the Greek society of that day was so totally convinced that women should remain in the background? Can you reconcile this with what Paul wrote to other churches, such as Corinth in Achaia? To them he made very clear that, though the gospel frees one in Christ, the women were never to be so bold as to do anything to bring disrepute on themselves in the eyes of their society. And we know that to exercise such liberty in Corinth would have brought disgrace on both themselves and their husbands.

But Philippi was not Corinth! Philippi was in Macedonia. And in Macedonia things were different. Here women had been granted by society a type of recognition that was enjoyed nowhere else in all Greece. And that freedom had affected the church. Turn to Acts 16 and 17 where we read of the penetration of the gospel into Philippi, Thessalonica, and Berea (all in Macedonia)—note how many women were involved in the founding of these churches.

So, as we see in our context, Euodia and Syntyche were leading figures among the Christians at Philippi. But the problem was this—something had happened to divide them. Some misunderstanding had arisen, and these two respected Christian ladies had quarreled! And it is apparent that their "falling out" had affected the entire congregation! Instead of simply praying God to give them a new baptism of Holy Spirit love, the congregation was being tempted to choose sides. The psychology of such a confrontation invariably forces the conviction upon both sides that somehow there must emerge from such a quarrel "a winner" and "a loser." Heels dig in and jaws set!

In our context, Paul is affirming that this type of situation should not be! He appeals to someone in that congregation whom he calls a "loyal yokefellow" and to Clement and "the rest of his fellow workers" to *help* Euodia and Syntyche to mend their differences *in the Lord.* The issue again is that the apologies offered and forgivenesses granted must be exchanged "in the Lord." Forced apologies and begrudging forgiveness would never have resulted in any constructive reconciliation between these two, much less unified the congregation! The "agreement" must be reached "in the Lord"!

I heard an evangelist refer to a church where this very type of situation arose. Two of the prominent ladies in the congregation clashed in a disagreement and hurt feelings smoldered. The two entrances to the sanctuary in that church became increasingly convenient! Instead of humbling themselves before the Lord and each other, both stiffened in pride. The one entered the sanctuary by one door and sat on the left side of the sanctuary. And when the service was over she would exit at the same door. The other entered by the other door, sat on the right side of the sanctuary and left by the opposite door. This practice persisted for years—as I recall, at least fifteen! One year the aforementioned evangelist came for special meetings. Each evening both ladies would attend. One entered and exited on the left side of the sanctuary, the other on the right. But down in the heart of each the Holy Spirit began to probe. The evangelist knew nothing of the situation. Neither woman betrayed the fact that the Spirit was melting her stony heart. One evening, unaware that the other was doing the same thing, each lady left her seat and knelt at the altar. And the one, weeping, begged God's forgiveness. At the opposite end of the altar the other, with tears of repentance, also implored God's pardon. When each realized the other was at the altar, they rose and met at the middle of the front of that church. With sincere apologies, they hugged, entreating each other's forgiveness! Both freely forgave the other and, with arms around each other, walked out the same door for the first time in fifteen years!¹ That is "agreeing in the Lord"!

As interesting as it might be to know whether Euodia and Syntyche ever so reconciled with each other, it seems we will have to wait until we get to heaven to find out. Let us hope they did. At least we know what the Holy Spirit desired of them, in that Paul exhorted them to BE PEACEFUL IN THE LORD. God help us to fulfill this practical injunction from the pen of the Lord's inspired apostle!

*PRAYER: Dear Father, we are much aware that it is so very easy to allow disagreements to blight our fellowship with each other. We pray that You will breathe upon us anew by Your Spirit today so that we will be able to maintain peace with our fellow man. We thank You for the privilege of having peace with God. Help us also to have peace with each other, in Christ's name we pray. Amen.*

WEEK 10:  Thursday
READ:  *Philippians 4:1-4 once again (give attention to verse 4)*

## BE JOYFUL IN THE LORD

Today we have read Paul's third exhortation to Godliness in this section. In verse 4 he says, "Rejoice in the Lord always.

¹I heard Dr. William Arnett, then Professor of Theology at Asbury Theological Seminary in Wilmore, Kentucky, give this illustration at the Prairie Camp in Elkhart, Indiana.

I will say it again: rejoice." In other words, he exhorts us to BE JOYFUL IN THE LORD.

If we come to understand anything from this epistle concerning the fine art of being a joyful person, we learn that such proficiency need not be dependent upon surrounding circumstances. Most of us already know at least one man in this world who seems to have the least reason to be happy—yet he is a joyful, buoyant, warm-hearted person. And, sadly, we probably also are acquainted with at least one person who possesses every fathomable reason to be happy—wealth, health, a good family, a loyal wife and a good home. Yet he is unhappy, self-centered, peevish, and ungrateful!

Of course, the opposite can be true also. Bitterness may result from the lack of material possessions—if one expects to find his happiness there! And one may be very joyful while enjoying material possessions, so long as he continues to realize that these are not the sources of such joy!

Paul, it would appear, recognized this fact as well. "Rejoice *in the Lord.*" There it is again! Our joy and happiness and rejoicing must have the Lord as its fountainhead. Otherwise, all attempts at "trumping up" such a spirit will be flat and extremely hypocritical. Do not lose sight of the context of all that he writes here. Paul, remember, is in prison. As stated in the last part of chapter 1, he did not know whether he was going to be allowed to live or be martyred. He knew that the Philippian Christians, too, would be endangered. It is as though he were saying, "I am saying, 'Rejoice in the Lord.' Yes, I have thought of my own circumstances and the possibility of losing my life. I have reckoned with the dangers you face as Christians! I have evaluated it thoroughly—and I will say it again: 'Rejoice.' "

Someone has said that, to some people, religion is like an artificial limb. It has neither warmth nor life; and although it helps them stumble along, it never becomes a part of them—it must be strapped on each day! D.L. Moody met a man at his hotel one day and asked him in his abrupt fashion, "My friend, are you a Christian?" The man stiffened somewhat and, with a half scowl, replied, "What do you think?" Moody replied, "Not a red hot one!"[1] That type of person finds it very difficult— almost embarrassing—to rejoice in Jesus! Why? Because the true source of that joy is not really on the inside. Under those circumstances, any attempt to "be joyful in Jesus" becomes a miserable bona fide success at fakery! Such artificiality always prompts more guilt and guilt drags misery in its train! It drives one into a vicious circle!

That is not to assume that a true believer always *feels* like rejoicing. It is to say that, as a true Christian, he has the right to recognize that he does always have a *reason* to rejoice whether he feels like it or not! And he possesses the prerogative to will to exercise that right to rejoice! David said, "I will rejoice in thy salvation" (Psalm 9:14). I maintain that every true Christian *ought* to be a genuinely happy person *by choice.* That is what Paul is calling for here. Christian, "rejoice in the Lord always! I will say it again: rejoice!"

These last three days, we have looked at three practical exhortations to Godliness. BE FAITHFUL IN THE LORD! BE PEACEFUL IN THE LORD! BE JOYFUL IN THE LORD! Let us, by God's help, choose to respond positively to these injunctions that we may practice "down to earth" godly living.

*PRAYER: Dear Father in heaven, You are our source of joy. When we know You through Your Son, Jesus Christ, we have the right and responsibility to rejoice in such knowledge! Help us to exercise that privilege today. Grant us Your genuine joy, in Jesus' name. Amen.*

———————————————•———————————————

[1]From *A Treasury of Sermon Illustrations* edited by Charles L. Wallis. Copyright renewal © 1978 by Charles L. Wallis, p. 59. Used by permission of the publishers, Abingdon Press.

*JOY IN A ROMAN JAIL*                                      161

┌─────────────────────────────────────────────────────────┐
│                                                           │
│     **FURTHER GUIDELINES TO GODLINESS** (4:5-7)           │
│                                                           │
│         **Be Merciful Through the Lord (4:5)**            │
│       **Be Restful Because of the Lord (4:5b-6)**         │
│          **Be Prayerful to the Lord (4:6)**               │
│          **Be Tranquil in the Lord (4:7)**                │
│                                                           │
└─────────────────────────────────────────────────────────┘

*WEEK 10: Friday*
*READ: Philippians 4:5-7*

## FURTHER GUIDELINES TO GODLINESS

I do not believe that we should ever conclude that the central fiber of living a godly life consists of simply obeying, in a perfunctory manner, the rules and principles of godliness. True godliness must go far deeper than that! Heart motives, inner love and proper attitudes all must enter the picture.

On the other hand, when love is maintained at a warm level toward God and when motives are pure and attitudes proper, we will *desire* to know the Biblical guidelines to such godliness in order to understand how our lives ought to be conducted. A number of persons have expressed to me on various occasions, "Life is so complicated and it is so difficult to know just how God wants us to act and react under so many given circumstances. If He would just write down on a piece of paper a set of directions and hand it to me from the skies, my problem would be solved." Well, He has not done that. But He *has* left us a written record with decrees, inspired by His Spirit, on matters which He felt were important enough to call to our attention.

In this section of Philippians, in verses 1-9, Paul has listed eight of those "guidelines to godly living." With these, two promises are offered for our encouragement also. On Monday through Thursday we looked at verses 1-4. In that segment we dealt with the first three of these exhortations. We saw how Paul encouraged us to BE FAITHFUL IN THE LORD, PEACEFUL IN THE LORD and JOYFUL IN THE LORD. Now, over the next four days, we want to study four more of these helps to godliness, outlined in verses 5-7. On Saturday, Paul will tell us to BE MERCIFUL THROUGH THE LORD. Sunday we will consider his exhortation to BE RESTFUL BECAUSE OF THE LORD. Monday we will hear him say BE PRAYERFUL TO THE LORD. And finally on Tuesday, he will encourage us to BE TRANQUIL IN THE LORD.

Before we consider these exhortations, we must be reminded of a very practical and important fact: though we may be full of the Holy Spirit, we will not come by any of these attitudes and actions automatically. Otherwise, Paul would have had no need to scratch out these lines at all. Because our natural human responses tend to drive so contrary to some of these principles, the Holy Spirit found it necessary to inspire Paul to write them, to be included in the Scriptures for our guidance and good. So let us respond positively, in yieldedness to God.

*PRAYER: Dear Lord Jesus, as we continue to study these guidelines to godliness, we pray that Your Spirit will implant in our hearts the power and the desire to respond to Your directives. We confess we need Your help, not only in the study of these verses, but even more importantly, in the fulfillment of them. Stamp these principles on the fleshly tables of our hearts, we ask in Jesus' name. Amen.*

WEEK 10: *Saturday*
READ: *Philippians 4:5-7 (note verse 5)*

## BE MERCIFUL THROUGH THE LORD

In verse 5 of today's reading, Paul exhorts us to BE MERCIFUL THROUGH THE LORD: "Let your gentleness be evident to all. The Lord is near." Scholars of the Greek language tell us that the word translated "gentleness" is one of the most untranslatable of all Greek words. The difficulty can be clearly recognized when we simply note the number of variations accorded it by the translators. It has been rendered, "forbearance," "considerateness," "humility," "forbearing spirit," "reasonableness," "courtesy," "magnanimity," "patience," "modesty," "yieldedness," "agreeableness," "pliability," "sweet reasonableness" and "moderation." One thing it does *not* mean—it is not a word that serves as an indulgence to sin. Such words as "moderation," or even "pliability" under some circumstances, or even "gentleness," locked into modern usage, tend to offer the concept of "permission to do a little so long as one does not overdo it." But none of that is to be found in this term as Paul would use it in a context of sinful or wrong responses to circumstances.

"The Greeks themselves explained this word as 'justice and something better than justice.'" They said that what was involved in this word ought to enter the picture "when strict justice became unjust because of its generality."[1] They would have said that a man has the quality expressed in this word if he knew when not to apply the strict letter of the law—when to relax raw justice and introduce mercy. But they must do so without condoning or indulging sin or wrong at all!

I believe one of the most graphic examples in the Scriptures of the quality found in this word is seen in the attitude Jesus

---

[1] From *The Letters to the Philippians, Colossians, and Thessalonians* (Revised Edition), translated and interpreted by William Barclay. Copyright © 1975 William Barclay. Published in the U.S.A. by The Westminster Press, p. 75. Used and adapted by permission.

displayed in John 8:3-11.[1] The legalists, who gloried in their justice, threw a woman, who had been caught in the act of adultery, at the feet of Jesus. They reminded Him that the legality of the law demanded that she be stoned. "But what do you say?" they asked. Jesus stooped, wrote on the ground, rose and said, "If any one of you is without sin, let him be the first to throw a stone at her." Then He stooped and wrote again. The men, ashamed, slinked away one by one. Jesus asked the woman, "Has no one condemned you?" "No one, sir," was her reply, to which Jesus responded, "Then neither do I condemn you. Go now and leave your life of sin." Or, literally, "From now, no longer sin." You see, strict justice, in that case, would have become injustice. Jesus knew when to relax the strict letter of justice and to interject mercy. And He did all without condoning her sin. That is what Paul is saying we should have as Christians. Call it "gentleness,"—but that is not quite it. Call it "forbearance"—but that does not cover it either. Call it "reasonableness"—that is closer. Maybe it is a sensible blending of all of these!

Now the fact is, it is not always easy to know when it is right to temper an unbending, staunch spirit with an honest sensible attitude of gentleness. Many see themselves as "tolerant" in choosing to compromise. Others imagine themselves to be "uncompromising" in their preference to be legalistic. Very few find it easy or simple to know how and when to be reasonable and gentle without compromise!

The only circumstance under which this concept becomes an issue at all must be when *morality* and *ethics* are involved. Take the woman to whom Jesus spoke—what she had done was, morally, very wrong! That is what rendered the situation so delicate and the response of Jesus so difficult to assess. But Jesus met the moral issue head on! "From now, no longer sin!" He simply tempered His strong uncompromising moral

---

[1]Though John 8:3-11 is not found in the earliest manuscripts, the consensus among many conservative Bible scholars is that this incident did occur during the ministry of Jesus.

demand with the mercy of forgiveness!

But what ought the attitude of a Christian be when a point of disagreement involves no moral or ethical issue? The Christian has not been invested with a blanket right to be bullheaded for the sake of "defending his own image." Three trustees, many years ago, discussed what color to paint the front of the church. Two wanted blue—one preferred green. So it would appear that the question was settled by a vote of two to one. But somehow that third trustee became obsessed with the idea that his spiritual valor would be threatened if he exercised reasonableness. He tenaciously clung to green, declaring, "I have to stand for what I believe." A regular trustee hassle resulted, complete with injured feelings. But where, in the name of sense, was the moral or ethical issue? There was none at all! And that third trustee became the long-range loser! He would have enhanced his true "spiritual valor" many times over had he simply and humbly exercised "agreeableness." And he would, most assuredly, have pleased God the more!

Paul says, "Be gentle." Why? Because "the Lord is near." We need to remember constantly that the Lord is "nearby" and observing all of our reactions to the circumstances of life. He completely "sees through" the veneer of our actions, and evaluates our motives involving those actions. Therefore, let us be gentle through the Lord. Let us allow true mercy to reign!

*PRAYER: Dear Father in heaven, You exercised mercy on our behalf when You forgave us all our sins. We thank You! Now, Lord, help us to exercise that same spirit. Grant us grace to demonstrate a right attitude of gentleness and moderation toward our fellow believers, keeping conscious always that You are near. And we will praise You in Jesus' name. Amen.*

## BE RESTFUL BECAUSE OF THE LORD

In today's text Paul exhorts us to BE RESTFUL BECAUSE OF THE LORD. Read again verses 5b-6: "The Lord is near. Do not be anxious about anything." That is to say, "The Lord is nearby, therefore, do not worry about anything."

I tend to agree with those who feel that the scholars who divided the verses of the Bible quite possibly missed the thought here. I find myself agreeing with many who are convinced that the phrase "the Lord is near" should not necessarily be connected with verse 5 (as we joined them in yesterday's reading) but rather with verse 6. "The Lord is near. Do not worry about anything."

Paul's intent here involves, not the nearness of His second coming, but His nearness to us in our present circumstances. So the meaning, as I see it, is this: the presence of the Lord is always near us who trust in Him, so we can afford not to worry about anything. In fact, since God's presence is so close by, it is wrong to worry about anything!

Paul Reese tells a story about 30 Russian peasants who, years ago, met to worship. Russia was under the regime of Joseph Stalin. Suddenly their worship was halted by the arrival of the dreaded Stalin agents. The leader barked an order to one of the other agents to record the name of every person present in the assembly. When finished, an old man spoke up, "There is one name you have not taken." "I have them all," smarted Stalin's man. "Believe me, there is one you do not have," the old man responded with confidence. A recount was made. "I have them all—whose name is missing?" At which the old man responded with a reverence that overshadowed the brashness of the hammer and sickle representative, "The Lord Jesus Christ, He is here!" "Oh, that's different," retorted the sneering agent. Paul Reese offers this final comment about the whole story: "It was different indeed—in a way, that Stalin's stooge could not possibly understand. The Lord Jesus, in sober fact, was there, utterly real to fate's eye, defending them with a kind of weaponry that munitions makers have never devised."

Oh yes, as the Lord was near those 30 Russian peasants, He is near to all who trust Him fully! Therefore, "Do not be anxious about anything." Did we read that correctly? About how much, again, are we not to worry? "About *anything*!" Paul is not calling for a shallow, foolish, naive attitude on our part which would deny the reality of danger or threat—he is simply asking that we recognize that God has everything under His control!

Nor does it mean that we err to ever plan ahead for such possible circumstances. A pastor had committed the unpardonable sin! He invited a house full of company and forgot to tell his wife! On Sunday morning he remembered and, with much embarrassment, told her what he had done—which made for a delightful atmosphere on the way to church! To top off the morning, his wife, who was desperately worried over what could be done now, was forced to listen to her husband, who had created the whole situation, preach on the subject, "Don't worry about anything, the Lord will provide." Inside she fumed with fury, as she smiled and graciously shook hands with the people at the close of the service. The pastor came home and, ushering his guests into the living room, found his wife in a rocking chair. No smell of food graced the kitchen. Now *he* became worried! At the appropriate time he eased up beside his wife and, as calmly as possible, suggested that perhaps it would evidence a show of wisdom if she would begin preparing the meal! "Honey," she responded with a sarcastic smile, "I have resolved to afford you the blessing of practicing what you preached this morning—don't worry about anything, the Lord will provide!" And she went right on rocking!

That is not quite what Paul has in mind in our text! It seems much more sensible to interpret Paul to mean that, while we put together complete preparations for possible dangers and

[1]From *The Adequate Man* by Paul S. Rees. Copyright © 1959 by Fleming H. Revell Company, p. 104. Used by permission.

threats, we ought not to worry about it! Trust all to Him! To worry is to confess that we really do not believe that God is big enough for that particular situation. The songwriter's pen scratched it on paper this way: "Why worry when you can pray? Trust Jesus, He'll be your stay; don't be a 'doubting Thomas,' Rest fully on His promise, Why worry, worry, worry, worry, when you can pray?"[1] And that thought leads us to the next concept which we will consider. Paul would say, "Be restful because of the Lord." And what next? "Be prayerful to the Lord." But we will take that up tomorrow.

*PRAYER: Dear heavenly Father, in all of the concerns which we face in life, help us not to worry. We trust in Your promises. Help us to leave our burdens with You and be restful because You are near. Thank you for Your wonderful promise, "Lo, I am with you always." Give us grace and wisdom to always believe that pledge. This we pray in Jesus' name. Amen.*

---

## BE PRAYERFUL TO THE LORD

Hand in hand with the meditation we considered yesterday concerning our BEING RESTFUL BECAUSE OF THE LORD follows our thought for today: BE PRAYERFUL TO THE LORD! Verse 6 says, "Do not be anxious about anything, but in everything, by prayer and petition, with thanksgiving, present your requests to God." John Newton penned his sentiments this way: "Come, my soul, thy suit prepare, Jesus loves to answer prayer; He himself has bid thee pray, therefore will not say thee nay. Thou art coming to a King, large petitions with thee bring; for His grace and power are such, none can ever ask too much!"[1]

The word translated "prayer" refers to what we might consider to be "prayer in general." The word rendered "petition," or "supplication" as King James has it, implies more "a specific type of prayer for definite and pressing needs." In our text, Paul pleads for both classes of praying! Do you feel that perhaps one of the reasons we have so many uptight Christians who do, in fact, worry away a lot of precious time and find it difficult to be restful in the Lord might be because so many pray so little? It sometimes appears to me that, to the majority of Christ's followers, prayer serves as a last ditch resort when nothing else works!

What does Paul say here? We ought to be offering prayers and petitions "in everything." Do we tend to think that God is not interested in the little "mundane things" of life? The fact is, most of our lives consist of one little mundane thing after another! That being true, it boils down to this—we tend to imagine that most of what makes up our existence is either not important enough to *us* to pray about or not important enough to interest *God.* Such thinking is based upon an entirely false premise and displeases God!

---

[1] "Come, My Soul, Thy Suit Prepare" by John Newton.

Paul is inferring in today's verse that nothing is too small to bring to God in prayer. The reason some Christians cannot muster enough faith for the "real crises" of life is clear. They have never developed the habit of praying and trusting God in the hundreds of "little insignificant agitations" of daily living. Let us present our requests to God "in everything." But let all our praying be seasoned "with thanksgiving"—not with complaining or bitterness or fear or threats to God! We are to be prayerful to the Lord. We are to be thankful to the Lord. May God give us continual help to exercise joyfully both attitudes!

*PRAYER: Dear heavenly Father, You know that one of the sins of Your people is that of prayerlessness. Grant us Your merciful forgiveness. Help us to pray more! But in our praying, help us to pray specifically, sincerely, and in faith. You are aware of all of the "little things" that we will face today. Grant us grace in all of our circumstances to be prayerful to Thee— and to be very thankful. Amen.*

WEEK 11:  Tuesday
READ: *Philippians 4:5-7 one final time (read verse 7 again)*

## BE TRANQUIL IN THE LORD

In verse 7 of today's reading, the following words are recorded: "And the peace of God, which transcends all understanding, will guard your hearts and minds in Christ Jesus." Paul's inference is that we should BE TRANQUIL IN THE LORD.

He speaks of a type of peace here which the human mind cannot either comprehend or manufacture. It is even more than "peace *with* God"—it is "the peace *of* God." God himself shares His very own peace with His people! And that peace, as God metes it out to us, "will guard (our) hearts and minds in Christ Jesus." The word "guard" is the same which means to "watch and defend" in a military sense. So it involves security, safety and protection—not only of "the heart" but also "the mind." Both spiritual protection as well as mental and emotional stability are afforded! Here is a type of spiritual tranquility provided through God's peace.

Jay Kessler, the national president of Youth for Christ, speaking to the youth of the Prairie Camp in Elkhart, Indiana, some years ago told of an incident that had transpired in his earlier ministry. He was to preach in a church in one of our cities. While seated on the platform with the pastor, he spotted a distinguished looking gentleman enter the sanctuary and slip down a side aisle to be seated. The pastor, leaning over, whispered to Jay, "Do you see that man? He is the psychiatrist at the local hospital for emotionally disturbed people in our city." Jay, still young in his ministry, became somewhat unnerved. He was concerned that the psychiatrist, instead of listening to the message, would attempt to psychoanalyze him while he was preaching. He said, however, that he preached as he always did. After the sermon, the man strode down the aisle toward him. Approaching Jay, he shook his hand and said, rather matter-of-fact like, "I am the psychiatrist at the hospital for emotionally disturbed people in this city. I just want to tell you, young man, that if all the patients with whom I counsel would experience what you have been talking about tonight, I would be able to dismiss fully one-half of them overnight!" Jay thanked the man warmly as he turned to walk away. And he rejoiced anew to know in his heart that the message he preached "really worked!"[1]

---

[1]Used by permission of Jay Kessler.

Now the fact is, God provides this stability and security through His Holy Spirit. But, in spite of such provision, some very unhappy, neurotic Christians have never learned how to draw on God's available peace. They have never learned how to *be* tranquil in the Lord. Let us allow God to give us all His grace to know how to *let* "the peace of God, which transcends all understanding, guard (our) hearts and minds in Christ Jesus!"

For the past nine days, we have been studying these first seven verses in the fourth chapter of Philippians. Paul has given seven GUIDELINES TO GODLINESS. Three remain. Let us review these principles. And let us ask God for His help to make them very effective and workable in our lives. Here they are:

1. Be faithful in the Lord.
2. Be peaceful in the Lord.
3. Be joyful in the Lord.
4. Be gentle (merciful) through the Lord.
5. Be restful because of the Lord.
6. Be prayerful to the Lord (with thanksgiving).
7. Be tranquil in the Lord.

*PRAYER: Lord Jesus Christ, Son of the living God, You are the fountainhead of a stream of peace and tranquility flowing from the divine to man! We thank You for such an abundant supply! You have strengthened us as we have studied these guidelines to godliness. Now give us grace to allow Your Spirit to work them into our very inner beings. And help us to live effective, growing, productive lives. It is in Your name that we pray. Amen.*

```
┌─────────────────────────────────────────────────────┐
│                                                       │
│         FINAL GUIDELINES TO GODLINESS (4:8-9)         │
│                                                       │
│            Be Thoughtful of the Lord (4:8)            │
│      Be Thoughtful of the Lord (continued) (4:8)      │
│             Be Dutiful to the Lord (4:9)              │
│            Be Trustful of the Lord (4:9b)             │
│                                                       │
└─────────────────────────────────────────────────────┘
```

*WEEK 11: Wednesday*
*READ: Philippians 4:8-9*

## FINAL GUIDELINES TO GODLINESS

These two verses which we will consider over the next four days offer Paul's FINAL GUIDELINES TO GODLINESS (practical exhortations to godly living). And he includes one final promise to all who will respond positively. To this point Paul has insisted that we, as Christians, should be faithful in the Lord. He has encouraged us to be peaceful and joyful in the Lord as well as gentle (merciful) through the Lord. He has said we can be restful because of the Lord. And we ought to be prayerful to the Lord and tranquil in the Lord.

Now, in the context which we will be considering in the next four readings, he concludes this total section of such exhortations by directing our minds to two final challenges. One involves our thinking, the other our acting. Or we might assert that the first appeals to our reasoning and the second to our responding—the first guides conjecture and the second behavior. His final promise then purposes to encourage our believing—our faith in the fact of the presence of the God of peace.

So we will be considering our thinking, our acting and our trusting. On Thursday and Friday we will see how Paul exhorts us to BE THOUGHTFUL OF THE LORD. On Saturday we will consider how he urges us to BE DUTIFUL TO THE LORD.

Finally, on Sunday, we will find that Paul prods us to BE TRUSTFUL OF THE LORD.

Now let us reread these two verses once again in order to prepare us for our next four days of study. And as we read, let us implore the Holy Spirit to make God's grace effectual to us that we may respond in a positive way to these practical guidelines to godliness. We do want our lives to veritably honor the Lord Jesus Christ, whom we love and whom we serve. Think, then, as we read: "Finally, brothers, whatever is true, whatever is lovely, whatever is admirable—if anything is excellent or praiseworthy—think about these things. Whatever you have learned or received or heard from me, or seen in me—put it into practice. And the God of peace will be with you."

*PRAYER: God of peace and glory, we thank You that it is possible for our minds, our actions and our emotions to be under Your control. As we study these two verses, we pray that we will be able to so submit to You that our thinking, our acting and our trusting will enhance Jesus in the minds of those who observe. Use us in Your service to help draw others to yourself. Grant our request in Jesus' name. Amen.*

## BE THOUGHTFUL OF THE LORD

Paul's first statement appeals to our thinking. He says we are to BE THOUGHTFUL OF THE LORD. In verse 8 we read, "Finally, brothers, whatever is true . . . noble . . . right . . . pure . . . lovely . . . admirable . . . excellent . . . praiseworthy— *think about such things!"*

We Christians do not always take seriously, I fear, our God-given responsibility to exercise the mind! The privilege of disciplining one's self to truly think is one tremendous God-given blessing! At this point, Paul is not referring at all to the idle rambling of a relaxed mind which many call "thinking." A more correct term would be "daydreaming." Someone has said, "Some people sit and think—some people just sit!" Over the door of the private library of Andrew Carnegie hung a motto that read:

"He who cannot think is a fool;
He who will not think is a bigot;
He who dares not think is a slave!"[1]

When Paul encourages us to the careful discipline of the thought-life, he is pinpointing the most important facet of Christian living—that which prompts or hinders all else! Jesus addressed himself to the activities of our minds. He said that it was possible for a man to allow his thoughts to so grip him that he could agree to sin in his heart without ever committing any wrong behavior outwardly. When the mind willingly consents, whether the actions follow suit or not, wrong has already been committed inwardly. On the other hand, Paul says in 2 Corinthians 8:12 that it is possible to have right motives in the mind

---

[1]From *A Treasury of Sermon Illustrations* edited by Charles L. Wallis. Copyright renewal © 1978 by Charles L. Wallis, p. 30. Used by permission of the publishers, Abingdon Press.

even before one has the ability to perform the right actions outwardly—and God accepts those motives. He refers to the giving of our offerings to the cause of the Lord and says, "For if the willingness is there (King James says, 'If there be a willing mind') the gift is acceptable, according to what one has, not according to what he does not have."

So what one wills to think *is* of vital concern in his Christian life! Someone has said, "You are probably not what you think you are, but you are certainly what you think." Another: "Sow a thought, reap a deed; sow a deed, reap a habit; sow a habit, reap a character; sow a character, reap a destiny!" When Frances Bacon was asked what he thought the outlook for the next generation was, he declared, "Tell me what the young people are thinking, and I'll tell you."[1] We may ask, "What is the future of the church?" I answer, "Tell me what we Christians feed upon in our thought-life, and I will tell you the future of the church!"

In our text, Paul paints an eight-fold descriptive picture of what the Christian's thought life ought to be. He lists each characteristic one at a time and then says, "Think about such things." Tomorrow we will focus our attention on these eight characteristics one at a time. We will see what ought to mark the thinking patterns of true Bible Christians. As we do so, let us prepare our hearts for examination and ask the Holy Spirit to test our thought lives that we may be certain they are truly pleasing God. May His Spirit help us.

*PRAYER: Dear Father in heaven, we thank You for Your thoughts toward Your children. It is our desire to think Your thoughts. We know that we do not always do that. Grant us Your forgiveness. We want our thought-life to truly be under the control of Your Spirit. Help us to think deep thoughts, holy thoughts, thoughts which will bring honor to the name of Jesus. And may such a pattern of thinking guide our lives*

---

[1]From *A Treasury of Sermon Illustrations* edited by Charles L. Wallis. Copyright renewal © 1978 by Charles L. Wallis, p. 277. Used by permission of the publishers, Abingdon Press.

*into actions that will magnify Jesus Christ, in whose name we pray. Amen.*

*WEEK 11: Friday*
*READ: Philippians 4:8-9 (look at verse 8 again)*

## BE THOUGHTFUL OF THE LORD (cont.)

Let us BE THOUGHTFUL OF THE LORD. That is Paul's theme in this section of his letter. And in verse 8, he enumerates eight characteristics which ought to be part and parcel of our thought patterns as Christians. We will consider these one by one.

"Whatever is true . . ."—this word does not only mean "truthful (i.e., the opposite of a lie)." The basic idea is more properly "real or genuine or consistent with what something is in its essential nature." The questions involving truth which we must ask ourselves are these: "Do our thoughts bring us to conclusions about God which are consistent with what and who God really is?" "Will our thoughts contribute positively to helping us be true (i.e., consistent with what Christ wants us to be)?" Jesus said, "I am . . . the truth . . ." (John 14:6). Let us honestly confess that much of what we call "thinking" is little more than rearranging our prejudices and preconceived ideas in order to stockpile amunition to more nobly defend our private concepts about God, theology, Christian practice and denominational tradition. Paul says, "Think on what is _true!_"

He goes on to say, "Think on 'whatever is noble' "—literally, think on whatever is "serious," and "honorable," or whatever is "respectable" and "invites reverence." Do the things which you and I allow ourselves to think about promote respectability and honor in our minds and in our lives?

Again he urges, "Think on 'whatever is right' . . ." Paul, I believe, would agree basically with one of my college professors, S.I. Emery, who used to say to us aspiring preachers, "Right is right if nobody does it! Wrong is wrong if everybody does it!" Does your thinking and mine prompt us to be and do that which is right?

A member of a particular congregation upset the entire worship service when he was observed to remove one shoe and then his sock. Asked the reason for such behavior, he replied, "I just noticed that one of my socks was on wrong side out. When I find I'm wrong, I always proceed at once to get right!"[1] Honorable as that may be, that is not necessarily Paul's intent here. It is not the persnickety performance of petty expectations involving outward appearances that counts! When Paul speaks of "right" he is referring to morality, to ethics! One may wear his socks right side out and obey all the rules and regulations of the church—and still be unrighteous! Being right must begin on the inside with a radical heart change by the new birth. A righteous heart will go a long way in producing right thoughts. And proper thoughts will, for the most part, result in a right kind of life.

Follow on to the next characteristic he mentions: "Whatever is pure . . ." The word used would basically call for "pure motives." Our thought-life must produce inner motives for behavior which are consistent with holiness and purity. But again, such motivation must stem from a _heart_ that has been purified by the sanctifying Holy Spirit. A pure heart prompts

[1]From _A Treasury of Sermon Illustrations_ edited by Charles L. Wallis. Copyright renewal © 1978 by Charles L. Wallis, p. 293. Used by permission of the publishers, Abingdon Press.

_JOY IN A ROMAN JAIL_ _179_

pure motives!

Connected with that we read, "Whatever is lovely . . ." He is urging that we think thoughts that will prompt us to behave among our fellow men out of genuine love. Let us be sure that we love our neighbor as ourselves. "So think thoughts which foster inner love," Paul would press.

Again he prods us with these words: "Think on 'whatever is admirable' . . ." Literally, "things that are worthy of praise." The word could hold the idea of "a good reputation." We who move in our religious circles are prone to feel sometimes that it doesn't really matter at all what other people think of us—all that counts is what God thinks of us! But we must never forget that our *reputation* will, to a large degree, determine how effective our testimony will be with others. That is why Paul is not only deeply concerned about God's thoughts of us, but also that we do not cause others to stumble either.

Joni, in her book, *A Step Further*, tells a very touching story. A young college girl had become a Christian. As a result, her thoughts and concerns turned toward her parents, for she wanted them to have the same personal relationship with Christ she had come to appreciate. But they didn't seem interested. For weeks she endeavored unsuccessfully to persuade her father to go to church with her. Finally, one Sunday morning he agreed. The service seemed to touch his heart. The people were friendly and the sermon appropriate. In the foyer he said to his daughter, "I must say that service today really moved me. Maybe I'll come around to seeing things your way in time. Just don't rush me." The daughter was overjoyed. As the family was getting into their car, a man approached from the opposite side and hollered a greeting to her dad. Her father turned to see one of the church elders whom he had met casually a few times at his place of business. "Good to have you here," he beamed. Then, as an afterthought, he added, "Hey, why not give me a call sometime and we'll get together and have a few drinks, okay? Well, gotta go, take care." As her father took his place behind the wheel, the atmosphere was tense. "You know," he said, "I thought this place and these people were for real, but they're no different from me." With that he closed his heart to the gospel and never discussed it with his daughter again![1]

What a senseless tragedy! At that point, the issue in any discussion concerning what had happened that Sunday morning absolutely cannot be whether or not that elder, as a Christian, might be free in his conscience to drink alcoholic beverages moderately or not! The issue goes much deeper than that. It involves the reputation of that elder in the eyes of a man who was trying somehow to understand God. The issue must throw questions on the shabby influence of that elder on a man who, at that time, desperately needed the type of example that was good and wholesome! What others think of you does count after all! Think about this!

Finally he says, "If anything is excellent or praiseworthy"—discipline yourself to think on these things! So Paul has spoken to our thought-life, and has called for the Philippians and for us to be thoughtful of the Lord. May God help us to guard our thinking carefully that the results of such will always magnify the cause that is pure and holy, righteous and true!

*PRAYER: Dear Father in heaven, we ask You again today to help us guard our thought-lives carefully. Help us to always remember that our thoughts do lead to actions—and that other people, some of whom are seeking to know God better, are watching our lives. We know that what they see will influence them toward good or toward evil. Extend grace that our reputations and our influence will always be for good. Grant our requests in Jesus' name. Amen.*

───────────────•───────────────

[1]From *A Step Further* by Joni Eareckson and Steve Estes. Copyright © 1978 by Joni Eareckson and Steve Estes, pp. 99-100. Used by permission of Zondervan Publishing House.

JOY IN A ROMAN JAIL                                              181

## BE DUTIFUL TO THE LORD

For the past two days we have seen in verse 8 the importance of disciplining our thought-life. We must BE THOUGHTFUL OF THE LORD. Today we will find that we should BE DUTIFUL TO THE LORD. In verse 9 Paul says, "Whatever you have learned or received or heard from me, or seen in me—put it into practice." He is directing us to the fulfillment of our everyday duties as Christians.

This is almost a repeat of what he had written in chapter 3 and verse 17. There he urged, "Join with others in following my example, brothers, and take note of those who live according to the pattern we gave you." Paul had lived among the Philippians and they had observed his life. It is apparent that he had instructed them, not only by precept, but by practice. He taught, not only by his word, but by his walk. He practiced what he preached! He could afford to call attention not only to what they had "learned or received or heard from him"—but also what they had "seen in him"!

While a missionary was giving a gospel sermon to some Hindu ladies, one of the listeners rose and made her exit. After a short absence she returned and listened more intently than before. At the close of his presentation, the missionary enquired whether she left because she was not interested. The Hindu replied, "Oh no, I was interested. I was so interested in the things you were saying that I went out to ask the man who works for you whether you really meant it and whether you lived it at home. He said you did, so I came back to listen again." Another young man was asked, "By whose preaching were you converted?" "Not by anyone's preaching," he responded, "but by my mother's practicing!"[1]

---

[1]From *A Treasury of Sermon Illustrations* edited by Charles L. Wallis. Copyright renewal © 1978 by Charles L. Wallis, pp. 112, 65. Used by permission of the publishers, Abingdon Press.

Now let us reduce all this to where we live! We, too, have learned and received and heard and seen what the gospel of Christ calls for in our lives. We are some of the most privileged people in the whole world! Most of us, on the other hand, wish we knew more about Jesus. We have moaned, "I just don't understand the Bible like I wish I could!" But that is not our greatest problem! We would have to agree with Mark Twain, skeptic that he was, who said, "Many people are troubled about the Scriptures which are mysterious and hard to understand. I am most troubled about those which I can understand."[1]

Everek Storms has recorded in an article written for *Emphasis* magazine what he feels are four of the greatest problems of the church today. The very first he subtitled, "The Problem of Non-Application." And under this point he says, "As church members, we have studied the Bible until we know all about it, but we do not apply its message to our personal needs." He continues by naming eight specific areas where he is convinced that we are guilty—then simply states: "Yes, we know all about the Bible; we can quote chapters from memory, we can cite texts to prove its doctrines . . . but our actions do not correspond with our beliefs."[2] There is our issue!

Paul says in our text, "What you have learned . . . received . . . heard . . . seen, put into practice!" In other words, "Be dutiful to the Lord!" Practice your duty!

Would the Lord Jesus have anything to speak to us at this point? I am sure He would. May we listen carefully to the tender voice of His Spirit and truly "put into practice" what we already know about God!

*PRAYER: Heavenly Father, we thank You for Your Son, the Lord Jesus Christ, who has set an example for us for our*

---

[1]From *A Treasury of Sermon Illustrations* edited by Charles L. Wallis. Copyright renewal © 1978 by Charles L. Wallis, p. 29. Used by permission of the publishers, Abingdon Press.

[2]From *Emphasis*, article entitled, "Some Basic Problems in the Church," February, 1979 issue, written by Everek Storms. Used by permission of Bethel Publishing Company.

*everyday living. Fill us anew with the Holy Spirit so that we may walk in that example. What we have studied today is directed to our hearts for our good. Help us to truly "put it into practice" to the glory of God our Father. We thank You for Your "everyday power" made available to us, through Christ, in whose wonderful name we pray. Amen.*

WEEK 12: *Sunday*
READ: *Philippians 4:8-9 one final time (focus on verse 9b)*

## BE TRUSTFUL OF THE LORD

In his last brief statement of this section, Paul intimates that we should BE TRUSTFUL OF THE LORD. He says, "And the God of peace will be with you." Back in verse 7 he had declared, "The peace of God . . . will guard (you)." Now he is saying, "The God of peace will be with you." In the first statement he stresses what God *gives*—in the second, what God *is*. The first stresses what God desires to *give* to His children. The second underscores what God desires to *be* to His children. And in both cases the desire finds its expression by the same avenue— the God of peace gives the peace of God!

The basic truth unfolded here is that His *peace* is made real by His *presence*. If His presence is with us, we have His peace. Here is the question of issue: "Can we simply trust His presence?"

Would to God that the simplicity of the faith and trust of children would be ours! As with the little four-year-old who crawled into the family car to sit in the front seat with his mother and father. "Scoot over, Mommy!" he said simply. "Why, Junior? There is plenty of room for all of us," Mother answered. His reply was matter-of-fact, "I know, Mommy, but we got to make room for God." I would that adult faith were so simple.

Now let us review Paul's ten guidelines to godliness one more time:

1. Be faithful in the Lord
2. Be peaceful in the Lord
3. Be joyful in the Lord
4. Be merciful through the Lord
5. Be restful because of the Lord
6. Be prayerful through the Lord
7. Be tranquil in the Lord
8. Be thoughtful of the Lord
9. Be dutiful to the Lord
10. Be trustful of the Lord

Possibly at this point it would do your heart much good to read the first nine verses of this chapter one more time before having a closing prayer. Why not do so for your own spiritual enrichment?

*PRAYER: Dear Father in heaven, all of these guidelines seem so direct and practical—and weighty! None is less important than any of the others. Each speaks its own challenge to our hearts. As we refer to them from time to time in our thinking, help us to purpose that they shall be made very effective in our lives. Give us grace, in Jesus' name. Amen.*

*JOY IN A ROMAN JAIL*

## ATTITUDES WHICH MAKE GIVING AND RECEIVING A JOY (4:10-19)

The Secret of Divine Contentment (4:10-12)
The Strength of Divine Enablement (4:13)
The Sacrifice Toward Divine Enjoyment (4:14-18)
The Supply Returned from Divine Investment (4:19)

WEEK 12:  Monday
READ:  Philippians 4:10-19

## ATTITUDES WHICH MAKE GIVING AND RECEIVING A JOY

Paul, at this point in his epistle, has finished with instructions, edicts and exhortations. The final fourteen verses are directed toward a delightfully personal matter which existed between him and his Christian friends at Philippi. The Philippian Christians had forwarded to Paul a special offering. Epaphroditus had carried the gifts from Philippi to Rome and presented them to him on behalf of the entire Philippian church body. And Paul's extreme gratefulness for their sharing spirit manifested toward him can be readily understood!

When these saints at Philippi had first been introduced to the gospel, they had responded with offerings. In fact, they were the only ones who had expressed themselves in such a practical way—none of the other churches in Macedonia had given toward the financial needs of the missionary party. However, quite a period of time had sped by and these believers from Philippi themselves had sent no further offerings. But now they had renewed that concern and sent an expression of their love for Paul once again.

In our text, Paul expresses to these Christians his deep appreciation for such thoughtfulness. In his comments, he offers four basic thoughts. Two of these express his attitude as the recipient of their offering—and, quite frankly, sometimes it takes more grace to be a good receiver than a good giver! The third and fourth are directed to the givers themselves advising what their attitudes should be when they give to the work of Christ. Actually, both sets of remarks may apply equally well to either giving or receiving, for he is addressing them and us as to what types of disposition can make giving and receiving a joy.

Over the next four days we will take a good look at these practical attitudes. If the frame of mind is what can make giving and receiving a joy, then we, as Christians, ought to purpose to develop such a proper mental stance through God's help. To-morrow we will study THE SECRET OF DIVINE CONTENT-MENT. On Wednesday we will examine THE STRENGTH OF DIVINE ENABLEMENT. Then on Thursday we will, hopefully, come to appreciate THE SACRIFICE TOWARD DIVINE ENJOYMENT. And finally on Friday we will note THE SUPPLY RETURNED FROM DIVINE INVESTMENT. Let us keep our hearts open and our minds alert to ascertain what the Holy Spirit would speak to us as we enter into this practical section of the Word of God.

*PRAYER: Our Father in heaven, we understand that when Jesus came to earth You gave all that heaven could afford for our salvation. We thank You sincerely! When He died on the cross He offered all that He had to give. Help us to under-stand that we are serving a giving godhead. From our study, enlighten our understanding that we may learn how to give cheerfully as unto the Lord. We pray this in His name. Amen.*

## THE SECRET OF DIVINE CONTENTMENT

Will we discover what makes giving and receiving a joy? First then let us learn THE SECRET OF DIVINE CONTENT-MENT. What Paul says at this point is expressed from the position of the recipient. But we may rest assured that it also applies to the giver. Basically he is saying, "I have learned to adjust to my circumstances." His present circumstance happened to be prison!

In verses 10-12, Paul thanks the Philippian Christians for renewing their concern for him—then says, "I am not saying this because I am in need, for I have learned to be content whatever the circumstances. I know what it is to be in need, and I know what it is to have plenty. I have learned the secret of being content in any and every situation, whether well-fed or hungry, whether living in plenty or in want."

Take note that he repeats twice the phrase, "I have learned." Though the original word in each case is different from the other, the idea expressed is the same. He did not discover this attitude automatically upon his becoming a Christian. He had to *learn* this secret! We tend to assume at times that if a person will just become a real Christian he will, in fact, be content. We develop doubt (to our chagrin), then, about some who do not seem to have found such contentment. And we tend to question the validity of our own conversion if we cannot maintain a 100% level of such satisfaction ourselves. Paul repeats twice that, as a Christian, he had to *learn* this secret to contentment.

Let us correct another misapplication—if we think that when Paul wrote, "I have learned to be content, whatever the circumstances," he meant he placidly accepted his circumstances without ever trying to change them, we are mistaken! In fact, the way Paul had ended in Rome had been the result of his refusal to be passive. He had been falsely accused in Jerusalem concerning his testimony for Christ. And he had appealed to the highest court of the day to fight that accusation! He had appealed to Caesar! And now he was in prison awaiting trial. Paul could have fully identified with what Bruce Larson calls "being risky Christians."[1] He certainly lived a type of risky Christianity. He was always willing to "take a risk" if it meant he could change some circumstance so the gospel could be preached with more effectiveness!

So what does he mean by the statement of our text then? I think the very meaning of the original word translated "content" exposes Paul's thinking. It is the word which means "self-sufficient" or "resourceful." Some circumstances simply cannot be changed—at least not at given junctures in one's life. Then one must learn "resourcefulness." Paul is saying, "I have learned to be 'resourceful' or 'self-sufficient' whatever the circumstances. I have learned to make what I have to be sufficient!" He had learned to "make the very best" of whatever those circumstances were! If he could not change them, at least he would not allow them to master him. He would mount them and ride them to victory!

In the early days of trade with Africa, a shoe company sent two representatives to the African coast to establish the shoe business. Both found the same circumstances—no one wore shoes! One cabled his home office: "You are wasting your time and mine. No one wears shoes here!" And he requested to come home. The other cabled his home office: "Send two boat loads of shoes—no one wears shoes here!"[2] Now that is contentment, whatever the circumstances! And that is the attitude which masters the circumstance and makes the difference!

So what is the secret of divine contentment to the recipient? I believe Paul is saying, "Philippian Christians, thank you for

[1] From _Risky Christianity_ by Bruce Larson. Copyright © 1981 by Word Books, p. 16. Used by permission.

[2] I sincerely wish I could recall where I first read or heard this story so that I could give proper credit. I cannot. I beg the indulgence of the originator.

sending an offering to meet my need! But whether you would or would not have so shared, I have purposed to be content! I have purposed to be resourceful with what I have and make it be sufficient. God will supply my need."

What then does he infer is the secret of divine contentment, so far as the giver is concerned? Well, the Philippians could have maintained, "We know there is a need, but if we give we won't have enough for ourselves!" Had they assumed such an attitude, it would have reminded us of some Christians in our day who assert, "I can't tithe! I just could not make it financially if I did!" Paul's insinuation is this: "You give to God's work. Then be resourceful and self-sufficient with what you have— God will supply your needs!" Let us all purpose to learn these secrets of divine contentment!

*PRAYER: Dear Lord Jesus Christ, we have come to realize that contentment is not only dependent upon Your attitude toward us, but probably much more upon our attitude toward You. Grant us the grace to learn how to be resourceful, and give us understanding that we may learn how to be sufficient with what we have. We thank You for promised enablement. Teach us the secret of being contented people. We will praise You because we are requesting this all in Jesus' name. Amen.*

## THE STRENGTH OF DIVINE ENABLEMENT

Do we really want to discover what makes giving and receiving a joy? Yesterday our study revealed something of Paul's SECRET OF DIVINE CONTENTMENT. Today we will discover that we must also draw on THE STRENGTH OF DIVINE ENABLEMENT. Read verse 13 again: "I can do everything through Him who gives me strength."

Again, I believe what Paul has written here applies both to the recipient and to the giver. In this context, the statement is made, from the vantage point of a potential receiver. He is saying, "I have been in both situations—well-fed and hungry. I've lived in plenty and in want. Neither situation need cut off the ability of God to work through me!" But again, his statment speaks to the giver also. Paul is saying, "You say you can't give." (For a period of time the Philippians, for one reason or another, had not shown their concern by giving—now they had begun again). Paul would say, "Yes you can—you can do everything or (anything) through Him (Christ)."

What is it that captivates Paul's mind here? He is zeroing in on the difference between the "I can" attitude and the "I can't" attitude as it involves the whole ministry of giving. But even more so, the entire vast difference between "I can" and "I can't" as it affects our *total outlook in everything* that is involved in serving Christ is in view here!

When it comes to developing a consistent attitude of tough confidence, we Christians are amazingly gifted in negatives! We seem tenaciously intent upon making it as difficult as possible for the Lord to do much of anything constructive for us or through us. We have been so habitually given to reminding ourselves of the utter helplessness of our estate that we feel it must border on "ambitious pride" to dare to think God might be pleased to do something "big" among us. True, we can never afford to overlook the fact that Jesus said, "Without me you can do nothing" (John 15:5). But neither can we afford to forget that He also said, "Everything is possible to him who believes" (Mark 9:23). Think of that thing (whether giving or doing) that you want to do for God. If you think you can't, you won't. If you really think you can, the chances are you will!

Sometimes what is needed is proper motivation. A young man found it necessary to walk home from an evening gathering. Darkness was settling, so in order to save time, he decided to cut across a cemetery where a freshly dug grave lay open. Not being able to see clearly, he stumbled and fell into the open grave. After a number of futile attempts to climb out, he decided to settle down until help came in the morning. A friend, also walking home from the same gathering, chose to shortcut across the same cemetery. Being a very excitable character, as he walked through the cemetery in the pitch darkness the strange sounds began to frighten him. His imagination convinced him that the best thing for him to do was run—you guessed it—he sprawled headlong into the same open grave. Heart pounding fiercely, he jumped and scrambled desperately, grasping for the edge of the grave! The more he jumped, the more he failed, and the more he failed, the more frightened he became! After a few moments his buddy stepped up and tapped him on the shoulder and said, "Hey, man, you can't get out of here"—but he did! Motivation, sir, was all he needed!

Sometimes all that is needed for God's people to look at a task with a different set of eyes is sufficient motivation. The eye of true faith, properly provoked, can see what an eye of doubt will never see. The Israelites and David looked at the same giant. All the Israelites could say was, "Goliath is so big, we'll never be able to kill him!" David, looking at the same giant, said to himself, as he picked up five stones, "He's so big, I can't miss!"

Now what is Paul's secret to spiritual success? Here it is: "I can do everything through him (literally 'in him') who gives me strength!" The secret is to be in Christ and to trust in His power! He is our source of grace and supply. What He wants is our cooperation. Start saying, "I can! I can!"

PRAYER: *Thou almighty Christ, we know that our true enablement to do anything comes from You. We have studied specifically that, in the matter of giving, our enablement is from You. Work this principle into our hearts. Motivate us to become good givers through the help of Jesus Christ, in whose name we pray. Amen.*

WEEK 12: *Thursday*
READ: *Philippians 4:10-19 once more (read verses 14-18 again carefully)*

## THE SACRIFICE TOWARD DIVINE ENJOYMENT

For the past two days we have been studying those attitudes which are necessary in order to discover what makes giving and receiving a joy. On Tuesday we saw Paul's SECRET OF DIVINE CONTENTMENT, and yesterday his appreciation for THE STRENGTH OF DIVINE ENABLEMENT. Now today we will see that, if we truly want to discover what makes giving and receiving a joy, we must give as A SACRIFICE TOWARD DIVINE ENJOYMENT. In verses 14-18, Paul reminds the Philippians that in the early days of his ministry in the gospel, no one shared with him in giving and receiving except them—not that he was looking for it, but he was looking for what would be credited to their account.

Now he had received their offering by the hand of Epaphroditus. And Paul calls those gifts "a fragrant offering, an acceptable sacrifice, pleasing to God." At this point, Paul's eye is fixed on the giver and the gift. And he is speaking to what ought to be our greatest desire when we give to the work of God. He is likening our gifts to the offerings and sacrifices which the Israelites of the Old Testament presented to God, and which were well pleasing to Him. He is saying that when we give financially to the work of God, our greatest desire, surpassing every other motivation, ought to be that our heavenly Father be well pleased! And, when we so give, we must recognize that, once offered, that sacrifice is no more ours but His.

Now the fact is, when we give to the Lord's work with the sole motive that He be pleased, He will see to it that we, too, are made happy and blessed. The happiest Christians I know are they who are consistently tithing, and cheerfully giving beyond the tithe that His work may progress. But the deepest issue is not your happiness and mine. The greatest issue is God's happiness!

Andrew Fuller, a contemporary of William Carey, helped launch the modern movement of foreign missions. It is said that one day he asked a friend in the community for a gift for missions. His friend responded, "Well, Andrew, I will give five pounds (about $15—worth about $200-$250 now), seeing it is for you." Fuller replied, "No, I can't take anything for this cause, seeing that it is for me you do it." Feeling the rebuke, the man hesitated a moment and then said, "Andrew, you are right. Here are ten pounds, seeing it is for the Lord Jesus Christ!"[1]

If our giving to the work of Christ is offered as an accommodation to men, the result will be flatness. But if on the other hand, we give "as unto the Lord for His enjoyment," the result will be fragrance. And, mind you, our own joy will also be

---

[1]From *The Adequate Man* by Paul S. Rees. Copyright © 1959 by Fleming H. Revell Company, p. 118. Used by permission.

full. Many are the Christians who can testify to the new found freedom they have experienced in Christ, and the joy overflowing, as a result of cheerfully giving to the work of the Lord —at least the tithe! And who knows how many have gone far beyond the tithe for the sake of God? They have learned by experience what Paul meant when he called their offering "a fragrant offering, an acceptable sacrifice, pleasing to God."

*PRAYER: Dear Lord Jesus Christ, in all of our giving to the work of God, help us to keep Your pleasure in mind. We want You to be happy with us. We want our motives to be noble and our responses to You to be positive. And so we ask for special help. Help us to give cheerfully. And we know that if You are well pleased, we will experience joy as well. Sanctify our giving to Your glory and honor, in Jesus' name. Amen.*

---

WEEK 12:  *Friday*
READ:  *Philippians 4:10-19 a final time (focus on verse 19)*

## THE SUPPLY RETURNED FROM DIVINE INVESTMENT

One more thought will enhance our discovery as to what makes giving or receiving a joy. We must come to recognize THE SUPPLY RETURNED FROM DIVINE INVESTMENT. Look at verse 19: "And my God will meet all your need according to his glorious riches in Christ Jesus."

A most difficult task for a Christian in America is that of differentiating objectively between his true "needs" and his "wants." The ideal, of course, is that we be so yielded to God that we will only want what we truly need. But that, as we know, is not always the case.

I do not mean to insinuate that it is wrong to express our "wants" to God in prayer. David said in Psalm 37:4, "Delight yourself in the Lord and he will give you the desires of your heart." Where did we ever emerge with the idea that God is interested only in our "needs"? I believe He is also touched by our "wants." And He responds to those wants, and fulfills them, according to what He ascertains is best for us, and according to what will glorify Him to the greatest degree. John Ogilvie maintains that God "provides our needs" and "redeems our wants."[1] We have the right to pray for both, ever striving to merge our wants and our needs into one. And we, of necessity, must leave with God the prerogative of answering our requests as He chooses.

In our text, Paul maintains that, since these Philippian believers had given an offering as unto the Lord which pleased Him, his God would, in fact, meet all their needs! Our "needs" is that to which Paul speaks in this section. The fact is we cannot outgive God. Not all of His blessings are given in dollar bills and real estate—but God is constantly in the business of returning to you and me more than we ever give to Him!

R.G. LeTourneau was one of the outstanding examples of his day of this Biblical truth. As a Christian, he founded a business which built great earthmoving machinery. But all did not go well and he found himself on the very brink of financial failure. In the middle of such frustration, God began to speak to him about tithing the income of the business. In his heart he struggled desperately! Finally, not without trepidation, he entered a covenant with his Lord that, though the business should skid to

---

[1]From *Let God Love You* by Lloyd John Ogilvie. Copyright © 1978 by Word Books, p. 157. Used by permission.

bankruptcy, he would tithe. He began to give faithfully.

For a period of time, though no improvement was seen, he persisted in his giving of one-tenth to the Lord. Then, wonder of wonders! Business began to take a swing upward! And the Holy Spirit asked him whether he was willing to increase his giving to two-tenths. He obeyed. Then three-tenths! Up to one half! When I heard him speak some twenty-four years ago, he was giving nine-tenths of all of the income to missions, the church, charities and to other facets of the work of God. And the one-tenth he kept for himself made him a very wealthy man![1]

Here was a veritable miracle of finance. R.G. LeTourneau came to recognize the supply returned from divine investment! Let us, too, be challenged by the fact that no one has ever found a way to outdo the giving heart of God. But let us also remember that, before He wants any of our money, God wants *us!* Let us give *ourselves* anew to Christ—and then let us give of our means to His work. And let us do so cheerfully as unto the Lord!

*PRAYER: Dear Father in heaven, we know that, when compared to God's giving, ours is so puny. But we want to give what we can cheerfully. And we want to give in such a way that Jesus Christ will truly be pleased. We do not want to give simply that You should return to us. But the fact remains, when we give, You do promise to supply our needs. For this, we are very grateful. Help us to use carefully what You give to us, knowing that all we have belongs to You. We ask this in Jesus' name. Amen.*

---

[1] I was privileged to hear R.G. LeTourneau speak at the Gospel Center Missionary Church in South Bend, Indiana, in 1959, where I heard him relate this testimony.

┌─────────────────────────────────────────────────┐
│                                                   │
│       **GLORY, GREETING, GRACE** (4:20-23)        │
│                                                   │
│            **Glory to God (4:20)**                │
│        **Greeting to the Saints (4:21-22)**       │
│     **Grace from the Lord Jesus Christ (4:23)**   │
│                                                   │
└─────────────────────────────────────────────────┘

*WEEK 12: Saturday*
*READ: Philippians 4:20-23*


## GLORY, GREETING, GRACE


We are focusing on the last four verses of Paul's epistle of joy. They include a benediction, a salutation and a final petition directed to God on behalf of the Christians at Philippi—and I believe on behalf of all of us. The manner in which he concludes this epistle is very similar to the way he closes all of his letters. His benediction, greetings and conclusion recorded in his epistle to the Romans are the most lengthy—a whole chapter of 27 verses! The closing of his first letter to Timothy is more succinct where he simply prays, "Grace be with you!"

These wrap-up remarks to the Philippians take on special significance when we are reminded one final time that they were penned from prison where Paul awaited trial in Caesar's court. I doubt that the scribe who had recorded what Paul had dictated (or Paul himself as he took the quill in his own hand to pen these closing words) realized that these lines would be studied by scholars long after the house in which the author was held captive, and the very palace of Caesar itself, had both crumbled in decay! Can you and I imagine the emotion shared between these beloved friends as Epaphroditus rolled up the finished scroll, tucked it in his tunic, and turned to bid "goodbye" to this giant in the faith? He had delivered the offering of the Philippians to Paul. He had listened carefully as he penned

Paul's dictated letter. Now, not knowing whether he would ever see his spiritual leader again in this life or not, he prepared to begin his journey back to Philippi—thankful that he was able to leave Rome without suffering arrest—deeply concerned as to what the future held for Paul. So far as we know, this was their final "farewell" to each other. Little did Epaphroditus know that he carried a letter back to Philippi that would help change the lives of millions of people of every age and from every nation that the world would ever bring into existence!

In these closing comments, Paul unfolds three thoughts which we will consider over the next three days. He expresses GLORY TO GOD which we will consider on Sunday. He offers GREETINGS TO THE SAINTS which will constitute our study on Monday. And he expresses GRACE FROM THE LORD JESUS CHRIST which we will read on Tuesday. Glory, greeting and grace! These are the thoughts then that will close his epistle. Let us trust, as the Spirit opens our minds, that these words will take on more meaning for us than they ever have previously. May God guide us.

*PRAYER: Dear Father in heaven, we pray that the glory and the grace of God will be much upon us as we endeavor to properly represent You today. We thank You for the provision of Calvary that makes such an unfolding of Your benefits possible to us. May our lives be a proper expression of these virtues. We ask this in Jesus' name. Amen.*

WEEK 13: *Sunday*
READ: *Philippians 4:20-23 (note verse 20)*

## GLORY TO GOD

In verse 20, which forms a type of benediction to this epistle, Paul ascribes GLORY TO GOD. "To our God and Father, be glory for ever and ever! Amen!"

I like the way Paul expresses himself concerning the deity we serve. He is "our God"—the one who is worthy of all of our worship and honor, our yieldedness, the bowing of the knee and the surrender of the heart! He is worthy of all of our love and genuine devotion! He is the holy one! the eternal one!

But He is also "our Father"—which speaks of the relationship we may enter with our God of a familial nature. He assures us that the distance between himself and man has been bridged. Though He is so great, so above man, yet we may call Him "Father."

He is our Father in a *creative sense*—that is, the general sense in which God is the "Father of us all." How is that? He created us! But He also wants to be our Father in the *redemptive sense*. Only as we are "born into His family" can God truly become our Father in this deeper, and more meaningful way. God becomes our Father, Jesus becomes our elder brother—we truly belong to the family of God! The song says,

> "God is my Father, Jesus is my brother,
> the blessed Holy Spirit is my guide.
> I am a new creation, the devil's no relation,
> I'm of the royal family in the skies."[1]

How wonderful to be able to call God "our Father"!

Now, what does Paul attribute to our God and our Father? "To our God and Father be glory . . ." The original word means "splendor," "grandeur," "power," "kingdom," "praise," "honor," "pride," "brightness," "brilliance," etc.—it is a great word! In his letter, Paul has thanked God for the witness of the Philippian

---

[1]The author of this song is unknown to me.

saints and that He had overruled his own imprisonment to advance the gospel of Christ. He has urged the saints to imitate Christ's example and to shine as stars. He has encouraged them to press on toward the final goal and to rejoice in the Lord. He has thanked them for remembering him with such a practical expression as an offering. But now he clarifies that all of the glory and honor for all the outcome of everything he has written belongs only to the one who has made it all possible!

Let us be very sure to perpetually retain this steadying thought clearly in our minds—especially as God helps us to grow in His love! The danger will always be to begin to feel "self-sufficient." The moment one tends to become "enchanted" with his own growth in grace, he will be prone to forget that it is only "through Christ" that such grace is made effective at all. All of the glory for everything good that happens in our lives belongs to God! The gospel songwriter, Fanny Crosby, penned it this way:

"To God be the glory, great things He hath done,
So loved He the world that He gave us His Son,
Who yielded His life an atonement for sin,
And opened the life gate that all may go in.
Praise the Lord, praise the Lord,
Let the earth hear His voice!
Praise the Lord, praise the Lord,
Let the people rejoice!
O come to the Father thro' Jesus the Son,
And give Him the glory, great things He hath done!"[1]

And I add, "Amen! So be it!"

So we see in this benediction that Paul expresses GLORY TO GOD. Let us, in our everyday lives, always be doing the same.

*PRAYER: Great eternal God of heaven, God of all glory, we thank You for salvation through Christ. We thank You for the fullness of Your Spirit and for His guidance. We thank*

---

[1]"To God be the Glory" by Fanny Crosby.

*You that God's glory is available to us continually. This day, grant that someone will see something of the Shekinah in our lives. We ask this, with thanksgiving, in Jesus' name. Amen.*

---

WEEK 13: Monday
READ: *Philippians 4:20-23 again (reread verses 21 and 22)*

## GREETING TO THE SAINTS

In verses 21 and 22 of this closing section, Paul sends a three-fold GREETING TO THE SAINTS: "Greet all the saints in Christ Jesus"—that is his own greeting. "The brothers who are with me send greetings"—here is a salutation from his fellow workers. "All the saints send you greetings"—so all the Christians in Rome join in the farewell.

This profuse expression of greetings is much more typical of the Eastern world than it is of the West. In fact, people of the East tend to think of the Western world as rather terse and lacking in warmth and feeling. And, of course, the Bible was originally written in an Eastern context. Paul practiced the customs which were common to his day and in his section of the world. One of these practices was the sending of formal and personal greetings to those with whom he had correspondence.

As missionaries in Nigeria, an Eastern-oriented nation, my wife and I came to appreciate this custom of lavish greeting

WEEK 13:                                                          *Monday*

much more than we ever had in our own Western culture. They greeted each other for everything! They took time for morning greetings, afternoon greetings, greetings for work, greetings for rest, greetings for sickness, greetings for the heat of the sun, greetings for the cold, greetings for sleep, greetings for weariness, greetings for tragedy, greetings for sorrow, greetings for happiness and on and on! And I confess, I came to actually appreciate the motivation for such time-consuming repetition.

Paul did not become entangled in as much detail in his greetings as do the Nigerians, but he did practice the habit of his day—in closing his letter he made certain that greetings were sent from "everyone with him" to "everyone with them."

"Greet all the saints in Christ Jesus"—even those who preached Christ with wrong motives as well as those who needed special encouragement to obey Christ—those who tended to be legalistic and those who quarreled—"all the saints"—the weak and the strong—all were recognized as saints and all received his greetings! "The brothers who are with me send greeting." Just who these brothers were we do not know for certain. Included were probably those brethren who visited him in his Roman prison—Timothy, Tychicus, Aristarcus, Mark, Justus, Luke Epaphras, Demus, Onesimus and others![1] "All the saints send you greetings (i.e., all the Christians in Rome)." But note: "Especially those who belong to Caesar's household."

Here were some of the servants on Caesar's staff in the palace at Rome who had become "saints." Have you been tempted to imagine that your circumstances in life are just too discomfitting to expect that you could ever live a consistent victorious life? Do you feel that your place of employment, your neighborhood, your business, your associates, your home or your circumstances just make it too difficult to live a true Christian life? Be informed, no one could have found a more demon-infested hell-hole in which to endeavor to serve the Lord victoriously than had these servants who worked in the palace of Caesar!

---

[1]See Philippians 2:19, Colossians 4:7-14, Philemon 23-24

*JOY IN A ROMAN JAIL*                                              203

Here immorality was accepted as a pattern of life. Emperor worship was forced. Christianity was considered "foreign" and "a threat" to Rome. Christians were immediately branded, and held as untrustworthy under the suspicious eye of Caesar. But Paul is saying to the Philippians, "Even in Caesar's palace are some who have been converted to Christ—saints!—and they are sending you their greeting as well as are all the other saints in Rome."

What can we learn from these warm greetings which close this epistle? Well, what is the real purpose of such greeting? It offers opportunity for the greeter to be a little more sensitive, and it allows the person receiving the greeting to become aware, in a little more personal way, that someone cares. No one appreciates the impression that he can enter among a group of people, spend time with them and depart—and never be noticed or missed! We all would like to be convinced that our presence has been noted by *someone!*

A simple, heart-felt greeting is one of the most effective ways I know to help others feel wanted and needed. Going out of one's way to recognize a friend or a stranger, a genuine hand shake on Sunday morning with fellow worshippers, an invitation out to lunch or to one's home for coffee—all of these, and more, can become tangible methods of greetings!

I am personally acquainted with a church where, for a number of years, one of the ladies of the congregation took it upon herself to prepare "a little extra" for dinner every Sunday morning. If visitors were present in the worship service, or people she did not know, she would invite them home for the noon meal! It was her way of "greeting new people." Sometimes her invitation was accepted, other times it was not. But the invitation was always sincerely extended, and true greeting was offered! This may not be your way—but let us all make it a consistent practice, using the method which best fits our personality, to "greet all the saints in Christ Jesus." In this closing section, Paul does just that in the only way he is able under his circumstances—by the pen.

*PRAYER: Gracious heavenly Father, Jesus cares for us! We thank You for Your personal interest in us as Your children. Show us how to care for others. Help us to be friendly Christians. Do not allow us to hold ourselves "aloof" or at a "safe distance" from other people, but grant us grace to become involved and to be the type of people who will be able to make others comfortable in our presence. Thank you for Your help and Your Spirit, in Jesus' name. Amen.*

---

WEEK 13:  Tuesday
READ:  Philippians 4:20-23 one final time (consider verse 23)

## GRACE FROM THE LORD JESUS CHRIST

On Sunday we read how Paul expressed GLORY TO GOD and yesterday we came to appreciate his GREETING TO THE SAINTS. Now today we will see how, in his final petition in his letter, he expresses GRACE FROM THE LORD JESUS CHRIST. Look at verse 23: "The grace of the Lord Jesus Christ be with your spirit."

In this instance, in petitioning the grace of God on behalf of these saints, and on behalf of all God's people of all ages, Paul's primary concern is spiritual. Read it again: "The grace of the Lord Jesus Christ be *with your spirit.*" According to the Scriptures, we are tri-partite beings. Our *bodies* give us world consciousness (we see with the eyes, hear with the ear, touch with the hand, etc.). Our *souls* afford us self-consciousness. Our *spirits* open to us an avenue to God consciousness. In the text, Paul's interest is that the grace of God will minister to and "be with" *our spirits*—i.e., that part of us which renders us conscious, on the inside, of God and His presence!

So what specifically is in the mind of the writer here? He doesn't say, of course. But I am satisfied that he is expressing interest not only that the grace of God be effective in working in us the new birth and the infilling of the Holy Spirit. His deep concern at this point is that we allow the grace of God to so minister to our spirits as to positively affect what we are *becoming* in the Spirit—our spiritual growth, the enlargement of our souls (understanding ourselves) and our spirits (understanding God). And it certainly would involve allowing the grace of God to actively work into our hearts a spirit of truly caring for the well-being of others, which would motivate us to put others before ourselves and selfishness into the background!

Now in wrapping up Paul's final thought, we dare not lose sight of the fact that this ministry of Christ to our inner heart and spirit is performed, after all, by His *grace!* "The grace of the Lord Jesus Christ be with your spirit." What is this grace? It is the unmerited favor Christ bestows—His gift of graciousness—the extension of help and mercy when none is deserved. So the apostle opened this letter wishing these Philippian saints "grace and peace." And now he closes the same by wishing them "the grace of the Lord Jesus Christ."

In these concluding remarks, Paul stresses glory, greeting and grace! Let us give God all the glory! Let us give each other all the greeting! And let us allow God to give us all the grace of His Son, our Lord Jesus Christ! So he closes this epistle. It is my hope that our study together has deepened our appreciation for the ever present and abundant grace of our Lord Jesus Christ! Let us read this treatise of joy often. And let us, along with Paul, learn to be rejoicing Christians, joyful in the Lord whatever our circumstances in life may be!

*PRAYER: God of joy and glory and grace, as we have read this epistle, our hearts have, in fact, been deepened. We thank You for its insights and enlightenment. We pray that, as a result of this study, we will be more loyal to, and joyful in, the God of our salvation. Breathe upon us afresh today by the Holy Spirit. Help us, whatever our circumstances, to rejoice in the Lord always. And we will praise You forever, in the wonderful name of Jesus, our Lord and Savior. Amen.*

# BIBLIOGRAPHY

## Scripture Translations

*Good News for Modern Man, The New Testament in Today's English.* New York: American Bible Society, 1966.

*New Testament in Modern Speech* by Richard Francis Weymouth. Grand Rapids, Michigan: Reprinted by Kregel Publications, 1981.

*The Amplified New Testament.* Grand Rapids, Michigan: Zondervan Publishing House, 1958.

*The Four Translation New Testament,* Printed for *Decision Magazine.* Minneapolis, Minnesota: World Wide Publications, 1966.

*The Holy Bible, King James Version.*

*The Holy Bible, New International Version.* Grand Rapids, Michigan: Zondervan Bible Publishers, 1978.

*The Living Bible Paraphrased.* Wheaton, Illinois: Tyndale House Publishers, 1971.

*The New English Bible, The New Testament, Second Edition.* Oxford University Press, Cambridge University Press, 1970.

*The New Testament from 26 Translations,* General Editor, Curtis Vaughan, Th.D. Grand Rapids, Michigan: Zondervan Publishing House, 1967.

*The New Testament in Modern English, Revised Edition,* translated by J.B. Phillips. New York, New York: The Macmillan Company, 1972.

## General Works

Barclay, William. *The Letters to the Philippians, Colossians, and Thessalonians, Revised Edition.* Philadelphia: The Westminster Press, 1977.

Clarke, Adam. *Clarke's Commentary, Volume II, Romans to Revelation.* New York, Nashville: Abingdon Press.

Conybeare, W.J. and Howson, J.S. *The Life and Epistles of St. Paul.* Grand Rapids, Michigan: Wm. B. Eerdmans Publishing Company, 1971.

Eareckson, Joni and Estes, Steve. *A Step Further.* Grand Rapids. Michigan: Zondervan Publishing House, 1981.

Ironside, H.A. *Philippians.* Neptune, New Jersey: Loizeaux Brothers, 1978.

Larson, Bruce. *Risky Christianity.* Waco, Texas: Word Books, Publisher, 1981.

Moody, William R. *The Life of Dwight L. Moody, Official Authorized Edition.* New York, Chicago, Toronto: Fleming H. Revell Company, 1900.

Ogilvie, Lloyd John. *Let God Love You.* Waco, Texas: Word Books, Publisher, 1978.

Purves, George T. *Christianity in the Apostolic Age.* New York: Charles Scribner's Sons, 1910.

Rees, Paul S. *The Adequate Man, Paul in Philippians*. Westwood, New Jersey: Fleming H. Revell Company, 1959.

Robertson, Ben. *Red Hills and Cotton, An Upcountry Memory*. New York: A.A. Knopf, 1942. c/o Random House, Inc., New York.

Spence, H.D.M. and Exell, Joseph S., eds. *The Pulpit Commentary, Volume 20, Galatians, Ephesians, Philippians, Colossians* (exposition and homiletics on Philippians by B.C. Caffin). Grand Rapids, Michigan: Wm. B. Eerdmans Publishing Company, 1962.

Storms, Everek R. *Emphasis on Faith and Living*. Elkhart, Indiana: Bethel Publishing Company, February, 1979.

Strauss, Lehman. *Devotional Studies in Philippians*. Neptune, New Jersey: Loizeaux Brothers, 1976.

Wallis, Charles L., ed. *A Treasury of Sermon Illustrations*. Nashville, New York: Abingdon Press, 1950.

Wesley, John. *The Journal of John Wesley*, edited by Percy Livingstone Parker. Chicago: Moody Press.

### Songs and Hymns

Crosby, Fanny. "To God be the Glory." Taken from *Hymns for Worship*, copyright by Evangel Press, Nappanee, Indiana, 1963. Elkhart, Indiana: Bethel Publishing Company, 1963.

Dodridge, Philip. "Awake, My Soul, Stretch Every Nerve." Taken from *Hymns for Worship*, copyright by Evangel Press, Nappanee, Indiana, 1963. Elkhart, Indiana: Bethel Publishing Company, 1963.

Lillenas, Haldor. "Emptied of Self." Taken from *Inspiring Gospel Solos and Duets, Number 2*. Kansas City, Missouri: Nazarene Publishing House, 1948.

Morris, Kenneth. "My God is Real," copyright 1944 by Hill and Range Songs, Inc., Copyright Renewed, assigned to Unichappell Music, Inc. (Right-Music, Publisher). New York, New York, 1944. Taken from *Favorites, Number Four*, compiled by Alfred B. Smith. Grand Rapids, Michigan: Zondervan Publishing House, 1956.

Newton, John. "Amazing Grace." Taken from *Hymns for Worship*, copyright by Evangel Press, Nappanee, Indiana, 1963. Elkhart, Indiana: Bethel Publishing Company, 1963.

Peterson, John W. "Why Worry When You Can Pray?" Copyright by Alfred B. Smith in *Happy Time Songs*, 1949. Taken from *Action Songs for Boys and Girls, Volume Three*. Grand Rapids, Michigan: Zondervan Publishing House, 1952.